Freshman Year Experience
Experiences for a Lifetime

Fourth Edition

Edited by

Eva Brickman
Deborah Thinnes
Barbara Osmon

Purdue University Calumet

Kendall Hunt
publishing company

Cover logo used by permission of Purdue University.

Kendall Hunt
publishing company

www.kendallhunt.com
Send all inquiries to:
4050 Westmark Drive
Dubuque, IA 52004-1840

Copyright © 2005, 2007, 2009, 2012 by Kendall Hunt Publishing Company

ISBN 978-1-4652-0188-1

Printed in the United States of America
10   9   8   7   6   5   4   3   2

Contents

Chapter 1

Touching All the Bases

An Overview and Preview of the Most Powerful Principles of College Success

ACTIVATE YOUR THINKING

1. How do you think college will be different from high school?

   _____

   _____

   _____

2. What do you think it will take to be successful in college? (What personal characteristics, qualities, or strategies do you feel are most important for college success?)

   _____

   _____

   _____

3. How well do you expect to do in your first term of college? Why?

   _____

   _____

   _____

   _____

Learning Goal

To equip you with a set of powerful success strategies that you can use immediately to get off to a fast start in college and can use continually throughout your college experience to achieve success.

THE MOST POWERFUL RESEARCH-BASED PRINCIPLES OF COLLEGE SUCCESS

Research on human learning and student development indicates four powerful principles of college success:

1. Active involvement;
2. Use of campus resources;
3. Interpersonal interaction and collaboration; and
4. Personal reflection and self-awareness (Astin, 1993; Kuh, 2000; Light, 2001; Pascarella & Terenzini, 1991, 2005; Tinto, 1993).

These four principles represent the bases of college success. They are introduced and examined carefully in this opening chapter for two reasons:

1. You can put them into practice to establish good habits for early success in college.
2. These principles represent the foundational bases for the success strategies recommended throughout this book.

The four bases of college success can be represented visually by a baseball diamond (see **Figure 1.1**).

TOUCHING THE FIRST BASE OF COLLEGE SUCCESS: ACTIVE INVOLVEMENT

Research indicates that active involvement may be the most powerful principle of human learning and college success (Astin, 1993; Kuh, 2000). The bottom line is this: To maximize your success in college, you cannot be a passive spectator; you need to be an active player in the learning process.

> Tell me and I'll listen. Show me and I'll understand. Involve me and I'll learn.
>
> —Teton Lakota Indian saying

Figure 1.1 The Diamond of College Success

The principle of active involvement includes the following pair of processes:

- The amount of personal time you devote to learning in the college experience;
- The degree of personal effort or energy (mental and physical) you put into the learning process.

Think of something you do with intensity, passion, and commitment. If you were to approach academic work in the same way, you would be faithfully implementing the principle of active involvement.

One way to ensure that you're actively involved in the learning process and putting forth high levels of energy or effort is to act on what you are learning. You can engage in any of the following actions to ensure that you are investing a high level of effort and energy:

- **Writing.** Express what you're trying to learn in print.
  Action: Write notes when reading rather than passively underlining sentences.
- **Speaking.** Express what you're trying to learn orally.
  Action: Explain a course concept to a study-group partner rather than just looking over it silently.
- **Organizing.** Group or classify ideas you're learning into logical categories.
  Action: Create an outline, diagram, or concept map (e.g., see **Figure 1.1**) to visually connect ideas.

The following section explains how you can apply both components of active involvement—spending time and expending energy—to the major learning challenges that you will encounter in college.

Time Spent in Class

Since the total amount of time you spend on learning is associated with how much you learn and how successfully you learn, this association leads to a straightforward recommendation: Attend all class sessions in all your courses. It may be tempting to skip or cut classes because college professors are less likely to monitor your attendance or take roll than your teachers were in high school. However, don't let this new freedom fool you into thinking that missing classes will have no effect on your grades. Over the past 75 years, many research studies in many types of courses have shown a direct relationship between class attendance and course grades—as one goes up or down, so does the other (Anderson & Gates, 2002; Devadoss & Foltz, 1996; Grandpre, 2000; Launius, 1997; Moore, 2003, 2006; Moore et al., 2003; Shimoff & Catania, 2001; Wiley, 1992; Wyatt, 1992). **Figure 1.2** represents the results of a study conducted at the City Colleges of Chicago, which shows the relationship between students' class attendance during the first 5 weeks of the term and their final course grades.

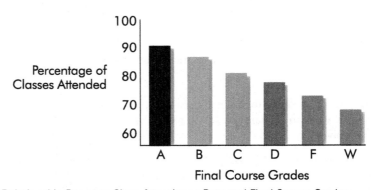

Figure 1.2 Relationship Between Class Attendance Rate and Final Course Grades

Time Spent on Coursework Outside the Classroom

You will spend fewer hours per week sitting in class than you did in high school. However, you will be expected to spend more time on your own on academic work. Studies clearly show that when college students spend more time on academic work outside of class the result is better learning and higher grades (National Survey of Student Engagement, 2003). For example, one study of more than 25,000 college students found that the percentage of students receiving mostly A grades was almost three times higher for students who spent 40 or more hours per week on academic work than it was for students who spent between 20 and 40 hours. Among students who spent 20 or fewer hours per week on academic work, the percentage receiving grades that were mostly Cs or below was almost twice as high as it was for students who spent 40 or more hours on academic work (Pace, 1990a, 1990b).

Unfortunately, more than 80 percent of beginning college students report having studied 10 or fewer hours per week during their final year in high school and just 3 percent report studying more than 20 hours per week (Sax, Lindholm, Astin, Korn, & Mahoney, 2004). In addition, only 20 percent expect to spend more than 25 hours per week studying throughout college (National Survey of Student Engagement, 2005). This has to change if new college students are to earn good grades.

If you need further motivation to achieve good grades, keep in mind that higher grades during college result in higher chances of career success after college. Research on college graduates indicates that the higher their college grades, the higher

- The status (prestige) of their first job;
- Their job mobility (ability to change jobs or move into different positions); and
- Their total earnings (salary).

Thus, the more you learn, the more you'll earn. This relationship between college grades and career success exists for students at all types of colleges and universities regardless of the reputation or prestige of the institution (Pascarella & Terenzini, 1991, 2005). In other words, how well you do academically in college matters more to your career success than where you go to college and what institutional name appears on your diploma.

Active Listening and Note Taking

You'll find that college professors rely heavily on the lecture method—they profess their knowledge by speaking for long stretches of time, and the students' job is to listen and take notes on the knowledge they dispense. This method of instruction places great demands on the ability to listen carefully and take notes that are both accurate and complete.

Remember

Research shows that, in all subject areas, most test questions on college exams come from the professor's lectures and that students who take better class notes get better course grades (Brown, 1988; Kiewra, 2000).

The best way to apply the principle of active involvement during a class lecture is to engage in the physical action of writing notes. Writing down what your instructor is saying in class "forces" you to pay closer attention to what is being said and reinforces your retention of what was said. By taking notes, you not only hear the information (auditory memory) but also see it on paper (visual memory) and feel it in the muscles of your hand as you write it (motor memory).

Remember

Your role in the college classroom is not to be a passive spectator or an absorbent sponge that sits back and simply soaks up information through osmosis. Instead, your role is more like an aggressive detective or investigative reporter who's on a search-and-record mission. You need to actively search for information by picking your instructor's brain, picking out your instructor's key points, and recording your "pickings" in your notebook.

See **Box 1.1** for top strategies on classroom listening and note taking, which you should put into practice immediately.

TAKE ACTION 1.1—LISTENING AND NOTE TAKING

One of the tasks that you will be expected to perform at the start of your first term in college is taking notes in class. Studies show that professors' lecture notes are the number one source of test questions (and test answers) on college exams. Get off to a fast start by using the following strategies to improve the quality of your note taking:

1. **Get to every class.** Whether or not your instructors take roll, you're responsible for all material covered in class. Remember that a full load of college courses (15 units) only requires that you be in class about 13 hours per week. If you consider your classwork to be a full-time job that only requires you to show up about 13 hours a week, that's a sweet deal, and it's a deal that allows

more educational freedom than you had in high school. To miss a session when you're required to spend so little time in class per week is an abuse of your educational freedom. It's also an abuse of the money you, your family, or taxpaying American citizens pay to support your college education.

© Joanne Harris and Daniel Bubnich, 2010. Under license from Shutterstock, Inc.

2. **Get to every class on time.** The first few minutes of a class session often contain valuable information, such as reminders, reviews, and previews.

3. **Get organized.** Arrive at class with the right equipment; get a separate notebook for each class, write your name on it, date each class session, and store all class handouts in it.

4. **Get in the right position.**
   - The ideal place to sit—front and center of the room, where you can hear and see most effectively;
   - The ideal posture—upright and leaning forward, because your body influences your mind; if your body is in an alert and ready position, your mind is likely to follow;
   - The ideal position socially—near people who will not distract your focus of attention or detract from the quality of your note taking.

Remember

These attention-focusing strategies are particularly important during the first year of college, when class sizes tend to be larger. In a large class, individuals tend to feel more anonymous, which can reduce their sense of personal responsibility and their drive to stay focused and actively involved. Thus, in large-class settings, it's especially important to use effective strategies that eliminate distractions and attention drift.

5. **Get in the right frame of mind.** Get psyched up; come to class with attitude—an attitude that you're going to pick your instructor's brain, pick up answers to test questions, and pick up your grade.

6. **Get it down (in writing).** Actively look, listen, and record important points at all times in class. Pay special attention to whatever information instructors put in writing, whether it is on the board, on a slide, or in a handout.

7. **Don't let go of your pen.** When in doubt, write it out; it's better to have it and not need it than to need it and not have it.

Remember
Most college professors do not write all important information on the board for you; instead, they expect you to listen carefully to what they're saying and write it down for yourself.

---

8. **Finish strong.** The last few minutes of class often contain valuable information, such as reminders, reviews, and previews.

9. **Stick around.** As soon as class ends, don't immediately bolt; instead, hang out for a few moments to briefly review your notes (by yourself or with a classmate). If you find any gaps, check them out with your instructor before he or she leaves the classroom. This quick end-of-class review will help your brain retain the information it just received.

Active Class Participation

You can become actively involved in the college classroom by arriving at class prepared (e.g., having done the assigned reading), by asking relevant questions, and by contributing thoughtful comments during class discussions. When you communicate orally, you elevate the level of active involvement you invest in the learning process because speaking requires you to exert both mental energy (thinking about what you are going to say) and physical energy (moving your lips to say it).

Pause for Reflection
When you enter a classroom, where do you usually sit? Why do you sit there? Is it a conscious choice or more like an automatic habit? Do you think that your usual seat places you in the best possible position for listening and learning in the classroom?

Thus, class participation will increase your ability to stay alert and attentive in class. It also sends a clear message to the instructor that you are a motivated student who takes the course seriously and wants to learn. Since class participation accounts for a portion of your final grade in many courses, your attentiveness and involvement in class can have a direct, positive effect on your course grade.

Active Reading

Writing not only promotes active listening in class but also can promote active reading out of class. Taking notes on information that you're reading, or on information you've highlighted while reading, helps keep you actively involved in the reading process because it requires more mental and physical energy than merely reading the material or passively highlighting sentences. (See **Box 1.2** for top strategies for reading college textbooks that you should put into practice immediately.)

TAKE ACTION 1.2—TOP STRATEGIES: IMPROVING TEXTBOOK-READING COMPREHENSION AND RETENTION

If you haven't already acquired textbooks for your courses, get them immediately and get ahead on your reading assignments. Information from reading assignments ranks right behind lecture notes as a source of test questions on college exams. Your professors are likely to deliver class lectures with the expectation that you have done the assigned reading and can build on that knowledge when they're lecturing. If you haven't done the reading, you'll have more difficulty following and taking notes on what your instructor is saying in class. Thus, by not doing the reading you pay a double penalty. College professors also expect you to relate or connect what they talk about in class to the reading they have assigned. Thus, it's important to start developing good reading habits now. You can do so by using the following strategies to improve your reading comprehension and retention.

Student Perspective

"I recommend that you read the first chapters right away because college professors get started promptly with assigning certain readings. Classes in college move very fast because, unlike high school, you do not attend class five times a week but two or three times a week."

—Advice to new college students from a first-year student

1. **Come fully equipped.**
    - Writing tool and storage—Always bring a writing tool (pen, pencil, or keyboard) to record important information and a storage space (notebook or computer) in which you can save and retrieve information acquired from your reading for later use on tests and assignments.
    - Dictionary—Have a dictionary nearby to quickly find the meaning of unfamiliar words that may interfere with your ability to comprehend what you're reading. Looking up definitions of unfamiliar words does more than help you understand what you're reading; it's also an effective way to build your vocabulary. Building your vocabulary will improve your reading comprehension in all college courses, as well as your performance on standardized tests, such as those required for admission to graduate and professional schools.
    - Glossary of terms—Check the back of your textbook for a list of key terms included in the book. Each academic subject or discipline has its own vocabulary, and knowing the meaning of these terms is often the key to understanding the concepts covered in the text. Don't ignore the glossary; it's more than an ancillary or afterthought to the textbook. Use it regularly to increase your comprehension of course concepts. Consider making a photocopy of the glossary of terms at the back of your textbook so that you can have a copy of it in front of you while you're reading, rather than having to repeatedly stop, hold your place, and go to the back of the text to find the glossary.

2. **Get in the right position.** Sit upright and have light coming from behind you, over the side of your body opposite your writing hand. This will reduce the distracting and fatiguing effects of glare and shadows.

3. **Get a sneak preview.** Approach the chapter by first reading its boldface headings and any chapter outline, summary, or end-of-chapter questions that may be provided. This will supply you with a mental map of the chapter's important ideas before you start your reading trip and provide an overview that will help you keep track of the chapter's major ideas (the "big picture"), thereby reducing the risk that you'll get lost among the smaller, more details you encounter along the way.

4. **Use boldface headings and subheadings.** Headings are cues for important information. Turn them into questions, and then read to find their answers. This will launch you on an answer-finding mission that will keep you mentally active while reading and enable you to read with a purpose. Turning headings into questions is also a good way to prepare for tests because you're practicing exactly what you'll be expected to do on tests—answer questions.

5. **Pay attention to the first and last sentences.** Absorb opening and closing sentences in sections beneath the chapter's major headings and subheadings. These sentences often contain an important introduction and conclusion to the material covered within that section of the text.

6. **Finish each of your reading sessions with a short review.** Recall what you have highlighted or noted as important information (rather than trying to cover a few more pages). It's best to use the last few minutes of reading time to "lock in" the most important information you've just read because most forgetting takes place immediately after you stop processing (taking in) information and start doing something else.

Source: Underwood (1983).

Remember

Your goal while reading should be to discover or uncover the most important information contained in what you're reading; when you finish reading, your final step should be to reread (and lock in) the key information you discovered while reading.

TOUCHING THE SECOND BASE OF COLLEGE SUCCESS: USE OF CAMPUS RESOURCES

Your campus environment contains multiple resources designed to support your quest for educational and personal success. Studies show that students who use campus resources report higher levels of satisfaction with college and get more out of the college experience (Pascarella & Terenzini, 1991, 2005).

Remember

Involvement with campus services is not just valuable but also "free"; the cost of these services has already been covered by your college tuition. By investing time and energy in campus resources, you not only increase your prospects for personal success but also maximize the return on your financial investment in college—that is, you get a bigger bang for your buck.

"Do not be a PCP (Parking Lot→ Classroom→ Parking Lot) student. The time you spend on campus will be a sound investment in your academic and professional success."

—Drew Appleby, professor of psychology

Your Campus Resources

Using your campus resources is an important, research-backed principle of college success, and it is a natural extension of the principle of active involvement. Successful students are active learners inside and outside the classroom, and this behavior extends to active use of

Student Perspective

"Where I learn the material best is tutoring because they go over it and if you have questions, you can ask, you can stop, they have time for you. They make time."

—First-year college student (Nunez, 2005)

"At colleges where I've taught, it's always been found that the grade point average of students who use the Learning Center is higher than the college average and honors students are more likely to use the center than other students."

—Joe Cuseo, professor of psychology and lead author of this text

campus resources. An essential first step toward putting this principle into practice is to become fully aware of all key support services that are available on campus.

OFFICES AND CENTERS ON CAMPUS

Several offices and centers at your college are designed to directly support your college experience. The following sections describe key campus services.

Learning Center (a.k.a. Academic Support or Academic Success Center)

An Academic Support or Learning Center is your campus resource for learning assistance to support and strengthen your academic performance. The personal and group tutoring provided by this campus service can help you master difficult course concepts and assignments, and the people working at this center are professionally trained to help you learn how to learn. While your professors may have expert knowledge of the subject matter they teach, learning resource specialists are experts on the process of learning. For instance, these specialists can show you how you could adjust or modify your learning strategies to meet the unique demands of different courses and teaching styles you encounter in college.

Studies show that college students who become actively involved with academic support services outside the classroom are more likely to attain higher grades and complete their college degree. This is particularly true if they began their involvement with these support services during the first year of college (Cuseo, 2003a). Also, students who seek and receive assistance from the Learning Center show significant improvement in academic self-efficacy—that is, they develop a stronger sense of personal control over their academic performance and higher expectations for academic success (Smith, Walter, & Hoey, 1992).

Despite the powerful advantages of using academic support services, these services are typically underused by college students, especially by those students who are likely to gain the most from using them (Knapp & Karabenick, 1988; Walter & Smith, 1990). This is probably because some students believe that seeking academic help is admitting they are not smart, self-sufficient, or unable to succeed on their own. Do not buy into this belief system. Using academic support services doesn't mean you're helpless or clueless; instead, it indicates that you're a motivated and resourceful student who is striving to achieve academic excellence.

Remember

The purpose of the Learning Center or Academic Support Center is not just to provide remedial repair work for academically underprepared learners or to supply academic life support for students on the verge of flunking out. It's a place where all learners benefit, including students who are well prepared and highly motivated.

Writing Center

Many college campuses offer specialized support for students who would like to improve their writing skills. Typically referred to as the Writing Center, this is the place where you can receive assistance at any stage of the writing process, whether it be collecting and organizing your ideas in outline form, composing your first draft, or proofreading your final draft. Since writing is an academic skill that you will use in many of your courses, if you improve your writing, you're likely to improve your overall academic performance. Thus, we strongly encourage you to capitalize on this campus resource.

Disability Services (a.k.a. Office for Students with Special Needs)

If you have a physical or learning disability that is interfering with your performance in college, or think you may have such a disability, Disability Services is the campus resource to consult for assistance and support. Programs and services typically provided by this office include:

- Assessment for learning disabilities;
- Verification of eligibility for disability support services;
- Authorization of academic accommodations for students with disabilities; and
- Specialized counseling, advising, and tutoring.

College Library

The library is your campus resource for finding information and completing research assignments (e.g., term papers and group projects). Librarians are professional educators who provide instruction outside the classroom. You can learn from them just as you can learn from faculty inside the classroom. Furthermore, the library is a place where you can acquire skills for locating, retrieving, and evaluating information that you may apply to any course you are taking or will ever take.

> "The next best thing to knowing something is knowing where to find it."
>
> –Dr. Samuel Johnson, English literary figure and original author of the *Dictionary of the English Language* (1747)

Academic Advisement Center

Whether or not you have an assigned academic advisor, the Academic Advisement Center is a campus resource for help with course selection, educational planning, and choosing or changing a major. Studies show that college students who have developed clear educational and career goals are more likely to continue their college education and complete their college degree (Willingham, 1985; Wyckoff, 1999). However, most beginning college students need help clarifying their educational goals, selecting an academic major, and exploring careers (Cuseo, 2005; Frost, 1991). As a first-year college student, being undecided or uncertain about your educational and career goals is nothing to be embarrassed about. However, you

© Monkey Business Images, 2010. Under license from Shutterstock, Inc.

should start thinking about your future now. Connect early and often with an academic advisor to help you clarify your educational goals and choose a field of study that best complements your interests, talents, and values.

Office of Student Life (a.k.a. Office of Student Development)

The Office of Student Life is your campus resource for student development opportunities outside the classroom, including student clubs and organizations, recreational programs, leadership activities, and volunteer experiences. Learning experiences in college can occur inside or outside the classroom. Research consistently shows that out-of-class learning experiences are as important to your overall development as the course curriculum (Kuh, 1995; Kuh, Douglas, Lund, & Ramin-Gyurnek, 1994); hence, they are best referred to as "cocurricular" experiences rather than "extracurricular" activities. More specifically, studies show students who become actively involved in campus life are more likely to:

- Enjoy their college experience;
- Graduate from college; and
- Develop leadership skills that are useful in the world of work beyond college (Astin, 1993).

Devoting some out-of-class time to these cocurricular activities and programs should not interfere with your academic performance. Keep in mind that in college you'll be spending much less time in the classroom than you did in high school. As mentioned previously, a full load of college courses (15 units) only requires that you be in class about 13 hours per week. This leaves enough out-of-class time for other campus activities. Evidence indicates that college students who become involved in cocurricular, volunteer, and part-time work experiences outside the classroom that total *no more than 15 hours per week* earn higher grades than students who do not get involved in any out-of-class activities (Pascarella, 2001; Pascarella & Terenzini, 2005).

> "Just a [long] list of club memberships is meaningless; it's a fake front. Remember that quality, not quantity, is what counts."
>
> —Lauren Pope, director of the National Bureau for College Placement

Try to get involved in cocurricular experiences on your campus, but limit yourself to participating in no more than two or three major campus organizations at any one time. Restricting the number of your out-of-class activities should enable you to keep up with your studies, and it's likely to be more impressive to future schools or employers, because a long list of involvement in numerous activities may suggest you're padding your resume with things you never did or did superficially.

Remember

Cocurricular experiences are also resume-building experiences, and campus professionals with whom you interact regularly while participating in cocurricular activities (e.g., the director of student activities or dean of students) are valuable resources for personal references and letters of recommendation to future schools or employers.

Financial Aid Office

Consider the campus resource designed to help you finance your college education: the Financial Aid Office. If you have questions concerning how to obtain assistance in paying for college, the staff of this office is there to guide you through the application process. The paperwork needed to apply for and secure financial aid can sometimes be confusing or overwhelming. Don't let this intimidate you from seeking financial aid, because assistance is available to you from the knowledgeable staff in the Financial Aid Office. You can also seek help from this office to find:

- Part-time employment on campus through a work–study program;
- Low-interest student loans;
- Grants; and
- Scholarships.

If you have any doubt about whether you are using the most effective plan for financing your college education, make an appointment to see a profession in your Financial Aid Office.

Counseling Center

Counseling services can provide you with a valuable source of support in college, not only helping you cope with college stressors that may be interfering with your academic success but also helping you realize your full potential. Personal counseling can promote your self-awareness and self-development in social and emotional areas of your life that are important for mental health, physical wellness, and personal growth.

Remember

College counseling is not just for students who are experiencing emotional problems. It's for all students who want to enrich their overall quality of life.

Health Center

Making the transition from high school to college often involves adjustments and decisions affecting your health and wellness. In addition to making your own decisions about what to eat and when to sleep, your level of stress is likely to increase during times of change or transition in your life. Good health habits are one effective way to both cope with college stress and reach peak levels of performance. The Health Center on your campus is the resource for information on how to manage your health and maintain wellness. It is also the place to go for help with physical illnesses, sexually transmitted infections or diseases, and eating disorders.

Career Development Center (a.k.a. Career Center)

Research on college students indicates that they are more likely to stay in school and graduate when they have some sense of how their present academic experience relates to their future career goals (Levitz & Noel, 1989). Studies also show that most new students are uncertain about the career they would like to pursue (Gordon & Steele, 2003). If you are uncertain about a career, welcome to the club. This uncertainty is normal because you haven't had the opportunity for hands-on work experience in the real world of careers.

"Among any population of young adults who are just beginning in earnest their search for adult identity, it would be surprising indeed if one found that most were very clear about their long-term goals. The college years are an important growing period in which new social and intellectual experiences are sought as a means of coming to grips with the issue of adult careers. Students enter college with the hope that they will be able to formulate for themselves a meaningful answer to that important question."

—Vincent Tinto, nationally known scholar on student success

The Career Development Center is the place to go for help in finding a meaningful answer to the important question of how to connect your current college experience with your future career goals. This campus resource typically provides such services as personal career counseling, workshops on career exploration and development, and career fairs where you are able to meet professionals working in different fields. Although it may seem like the beginning of your career is light-years away because you're just starting college, the process of exploring, planning, and preparing for career success begins in the first year of college.

TOUCHING THE THIRD BASE OF COLLEGE SUCCESS: INTERPERSONAL INTERACTION AND COLLABORATION

Pause for Reflection

Look back at the major campus resources that have been mentioned in this section. Which two or three of them do you think you should use immediately?

Why have you identified these resources as your top priorities at this time?

Consider asking your course instructor or academic advisor for recommendations about what campus resources you should consult during your first term on campus.

Learning is strengthened when it takes place in a social context that involves interpersonal interaction. As some scholars put it, human knowledge is socially constructed, or built through interaction and dialogue with others. According to these scholars, your interpersonal conversations become mentally internalized (represented in your mind) and are shaped by the dialogue you've had with others (Bruffee, 1993). Thus, by having frequent, intelligent conversations with others, you broaden your knowledge and deepen your thinking.

Four particular forms of interpersonal interaction have been found to be strongly associated with student learning and motivation in college:

1. Student–faculty interaction
2. Student–advisor interaction
3. Student–mentor interaction
4. Student–student (peer) interaction

Interaction with Faculty Members

Studies repeatedly show that college success is influenced heavily by the quality and quantity of student–faculty interaction *outside the classroom*. Such contact is positively associated with the following positive outcomes for college students:

- Improved academic performance;
- Increased critical thinking skills;
- Greater satisfaction with the college experience;
- Increased likelihood of completing a college degree; and
- Stronger desire to seek education beyond college (Astin, 1993; Pascarella & Terenzini, 1991, 2005).

These positive results are so strong and widespread that we encourage you to seek interaction with college faculty outside of class time. Here are some of the most manageable ways to increase your out-of-class contact with college instructors during the first year of college.

1. Approach your instructors immediately after class.

If you are interested in talking about something that was just discussed in class, your instructor will likely be most interested in discussing it with you as soon as the class session ends. Furthermore, interaction with your instructor immediately after class can help the professor get to know you as an individual, which should increase your confidence and willingness to seek subsequent contact.

2. Seek interaction with your course instructors during their office hours.

One of the most important pieces of information on a course syllabus is your instructor's office hours. Make note of these office hours, and make an earnest attempt to capitalize on them. College professors spend most of their professional time outside the classroom preparing for class, grading papers, conducting research, and serving on college committees. However, some of their out-of-class time is reserved specifically for office hours during which they are expected to be available.

You can schedule an office visit with your instructor during the early stages of the course. You can use this time to discuss course assignments, term-paper topics, and career options in your instructor's field. Try to make at least one visit to the office of each of your instructors, preferably early in the term, when quality time is easier to find, rather than at midterm, when major exams and assignments begin to pile up.

Even if your early contact with instructors is only for a few minutes, it can be a valuable icebreaker that helps your instructors get to know you as a person and helps you feel more comfortable interacting with them in the future.

3. Contact your instructors through e-mail.

Electronic communication is another effective way to interact with an instructor, particularly if that professor's office hours conflict with your class schedule, work responsibilities, or family commitments. If you are a commuter student who does not live on campus, or if you are an adult student who is juggling family and work commitments and your academic schedule, e-mail communication may be an especially effective and efficient mode of interaction for you. If you're shy or hesitant about "invading" your professor's office space, e-mail can provide a less threatening way to interact and may give you the self-confidence to seek face-to-face contact with an instructor. In one national survey, almost half of college students reported that e-mail has allowed them to communicate their ideas with professors on subjects that they would not have discussed in person (Pew Internet & American Life Project, 2002).

Student Perspective

"I wish that I would have taken advantage of professors' open-door policies when I had questions, because actually understanding what I was doing, instead of guessing, would have saved me a lot of stress and re-doing what I did wrong the first time."

—College sophomore (Walsh, 2005)

Interaction with an Advisor

An academic advisor can be an effective referral agent who can direct you to, and connect you with, campus support services that best meet your needs. An advisor can also help you understand college procedures and navigate the bureaucratic maze of college policies and politics.

Remember

An academic advisor is not someone you see just once per term when you need to get a signature for class scheduling and course registration. An advisor is someone you should visit more regularly than your course instructors. Your instructors will change from term to term, but your academic advisor may be the one professional on campus with whom you have regular contact and a stable, ongoing relationship throughout your college experience.

Your academic advisor should be someone whom you feel comfortable speaking with, someone who knows your name, and someone who's familiar with your personal interests and abilities. Give your advisor the opportunity to get to know you personally, and seek your advisor's input on courses, majors, and personal issues that may be affecting your academic performance.

Pause for Reflection

Do you have a personally assigned advisor?

If yes, do you know who this person is and where he or she can be found?

If no, do you know where to go if you have questions about your class schedule or academic plans?

If you have been assigned an advisor and you find that you cannot develop a good relationship with this person, ask the director of advising or academic dean if you could be assigned to someone else. Ask other students about their advising experience and whether they know any advisors they can recommend to you.

If your college does not assign you a personal advisor but offers drop-by or drop-in advising, you may see a different advisor each time you visit the center. If you are not satisfied with this system of multiple advisors, find one advisor with whom you feel most comfortable and make that person your personal advisor by scheduling your appointments in advance. This will enable you to consistently connect with the same advisor and develop an ongoing relationship.

Interaction with a Mentor

A mentor may be described as an experienced guide who takes personal interest in you and the progress you're making toward your goals. (For example, in the movie *Star Wars*, Yoda served as a mentor for Luke Skywalker.) Research in higher education demonstrates that a mentor can make first-year students feel significant and enable them to stay on track until they complete their college degree (Campbell & Campbell, 1997; Knox, 2008). A mentor can assist you in troubleshooting difficult or complicated issues that you may not be able to resolve on your own and is someone with whom you can share good news, such as your success stories and personal accomplishments. Look for someone on campus with whom you can develop this type of trusting relationship. Many people on campus have the potential to be outstanding mentors, including the following:

- Your instructor in a first-year seminar or experience course
- Faculty in your intended major
- Juniors, seniors, or graduate students in your intended field of study
- Working professionals in careers that interest you
- Academic support professionals (e.g., professional tutors in the Learning Center)
- Career counselors
- Personal counselors
- Learning assistance professionals (e.g., from the Learning Center)
- Student development professionals (e.g., the director of student life or residential life)
- Campus minister or chaplain
- Financial aid counselors or advisor

Interaction with Peers (Student–Student Interaction)

Studies of college students repeatedly point to the power of the peer group as a source of social and academic support (Pascarella, 2005). One study of more than 25,000 college students revealed that when peers interact with one another while learning they achieve higher levels of academic performance and are more likely to persist to degree completion (Astin, 1993). In another study that involved in-depth interviews with more than 1,600 college students, it was discovered that almost all students who struggled academically had one particular study habit in common: They always studied alone (Light, 2001).

Peer interaction is especially important during the first term of college. At this stage of the college experience, new students have a strong need for belongingness and social acceptance because many of them have just left the lifelong security of family and hometown friends. As a new student, it may be useful to view your early stage of the college experience and academic performance in terms of the classic hierarchy model of human needs, developed by American psychologist Abraham Maslow (see **Figure 1.3**).

© Monkey Business Images, 2010. Under license from Shutterstock, Inc.

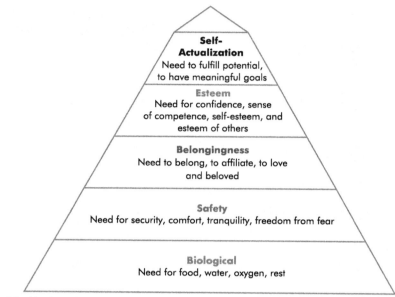

Figure 1.3 Abraham Maslow's Hierarchy of Needs Resembles a Pyramid

According to Maslow's model, humans cannot reach their full potential and achieve peak performance until their more basic emotional and social needs have been met (e.g., their needs for personal safety, social acceptance, and self-esteem). Making early connections with your peers helps you meet these basic human needs, provides you with a base of social support to ease your integration into the college community, and prepares you to move up to higher levels of the need hierarchy (e.g., achieving educational excellence and fulfilling your potential).

Studies repeatedly show that students who become socially integrated or connected with other members of the college community are more likely to complete their first year of college and continue on to complete their college degree (Tinto, 1993). (For effective ways to make these interpersonal connections, see **Box 1.3.**)

Getting involved with campus organizations or activities is one way to connect you with other students. Also, try to interact with students who have spent more time at college than you. Sophomores, juniors, and seniors can be valuable social resources for a new student. You're likely to find that they are willing to share their experiences with you because you have shown an interest in hearing what they have to say. You may even be the first person who has bothered to ask them what their experiences have been like on your campus. You can learn from their experiences by asking them which courses and instructors they would recommend or what advisors they found to be most well informed and personable.

TAKE ACTION 1.3—MAKING CONNECTIONS WITH MEMBERS OF YOUR COLLEGE COMMUNITY

Consider 10 tips for making important interpersonal connections in college. Start making these connections now so that you can begin constructing a base of social support that will strengthen your performance during your first term and, perhaps, throughout your college experience.

1. Connect with a favorite peer or student development professional that you may have met during orientation.

2. Connect with peers who live near you or who commute to school from the same community in which you live. If your schedules are similar, consider carpooling together.

3. Join a college club, student organization, campus committee, intramural team, or volunteer-service group whose members may share the same personal or career interests as you.

4. Connect with a peer leader who has been trained to assist new students (e.g., peer tutor, peer mentor, or peer counselor) or with a peer who has more college experience than you (e.g., sophomore, junior, or senior).

5. Look for and connect with a motivated classmate in each of your classes, and try working as a team to take notes, complete reading assignments, and study for exams. (Look especially to team up with a peer who may be in more than one class with you.)

6. Connect with faculty members in a field that you're considering as a major by visiting them during office hours, conversing briefly with them after class, or communicating with them via e-mail.

7. Connect with an academic support professional in your college's Learning Center for personalized academic assistance or tutoring related to any course in which you'd like to improve your performance.

8. Connect with an academic advisor to discuss and develop your educational plans.

9. Connect with a college librarian to get early assistance and a head start on any research project that you've been assigned.

10. Connect with a personal counselor or campus minister to discuss any college-adjustment or personal-life issues that you may be experiencing.

Remember

Your peers can be more than competitors or a source of negative peer pressure; they can also be collaborators, a source of positive social influence, and a resource for college success. Be on the lookout for classmates who are motivated to learn and willing to learn with you, and keep an eye out for advanced students who are willing to assist you. Start building your social-support network by surrounding yourself with success-seeking and success-achieving students. They can be a stimulating source of positive peer power that drives you to higher levels of academic performance and heightens your motivational drive to complete college.

Collaboration with Peers

> "**TEAM** = **T**ogether **E**veryone **A**chieves **M**ore"
>
> —Author unknown

Simply defined, collaboration is the process of two or more people working interdependently toward a common goal (as opposed to working independently or competitively). Collaboration involves true teamwork, in which teammates support one another's success and take equal responsibility for helping the team move toward its shared goal. Research on students from kindergarten through college shows that when students collaborate in teams their academic performance and interpersonal skills improve dramatically (Cuseo, 1996).

To maximize the power of collaboration, use the following guidelines to make wise choices about teammates who will contribute positively to the quality and productivity of your learning team:

> "Surround yourself with only people who are going to lift you higher."
>
> —Oprah Winfrey, actress and talk-show host

1. Observe your classmates with an eye toward identifying potentially good teammates. Look for fellow students who are motivated and who will likely contribute to your team's success, rather than those whom you suspect may just be hitchhikers looking for a free ride.

2. Don't team up exclusively with peers who are similar to you in terms of their personal characteristics, backgrounds, and experiences. Instead, include teammates who differ from you in age; gender; ethnic, racial, cultural or geographical background; learning style; and personality characteristics. Such variety brings different life experiences, styles of thinking, and learning strategies to your team, which enrich not only its diversity but its quality as well. If your team consists only of friends or classmates whose interests and lifestyles are similar to your own, this familiarity can interfere with your team's focus and performance because your common experiences can get you off track and on to topics that have nothing to do with the learning task (e.g., what you did last weekend or what you are planning to do next weekend).

Remember

Seek diversity; capitalize on the advantages of collaborating with peers with varied backgrounds and lifestyles. Simply stated, studies show that we learn more from people who are different from us than we do from people who are similar to us (Pascarella, 2001).

Keep in mind that learning teams are not simply study groups formed the night before an exam. Effective learning teams collaborate more regularly and work on more varied academic tasks than late-night study groups. For example, you can form note-taking teams, reading teams, or test results-reviews teams.

TOUCHING THE FOURTH (HOME) BASE OF COLLEGE SUCCESS: PERSONAL REFLECTION AND SELF-AWARENESS

The final steps in the learning process, whether it be learning in the classroom or learning from experience, are to step back from the process, thoughtfully review it, and connect it to what you already know. Reflection may be defined as the flip side of active involvement; both processes are necessary for learning to be complete. Learning requires not only effortful action but also thoughtful reflection. Active involvement gets and holds your focus of attention, which enables information to reach your brain, and personal reflection promotes consolidation, which locks that information into your brain's long-term memory (Bligh, 2000; Broadbent, 1970). Brain research reveals that two brain-wave patterns are associated with the mental states of involvement and reflection (Bradshaw, 1995). The brain-wave

Pause for Reflection

Think about the students in your classes this term. Are there any students who you might want to join with to form learning teams?

Do you have any classmates who are in more than one class with you and who might be good peer partners for the courses you have in common?

pattern on the left in **Figure 1.4** reveal faster activity, indicating that the person is actively involved in the learning task and attending to it. The slower brain-wave pattern on the right in the figure indicates that the person is thinking deeply about information taken in, which will help consolidate or lock that information into long-term memory. Thus, effective learning combines active mental involvement (characterized by faster, shorter brain waves) with thoughtful reflection (characterized by slower, longer brain waves).

Faster Brain-Wave Pattern Associated with a Mental State of *Active Involvement*

Slower Brain-Wave Pattern Associated with a Mental State of *Reflective Thinking*

Figure 1.4

Personal reflection involves introspection—turning inward and inspecting yourself to gain deeper self-awareness of what you've done, what you're doing, or what you intend to do. Two forms of self-awareness are particularly important for success in college:

1. Self-assessment
2. Self-monitoring

"We learn to do neither by thinking nor by doing; we learn to do by thinking about what we are doing."

—George Stoddard, former professor of psychology and education at the University of Iowa

Self-Assessment

Simply defined, self-assessment is the process of reflecting on and evaluating your personal characteristics, such as your personality traits, learning habits, and strengths or weaknesses. Self-assessment promotes self-awareness, which is the critical first step in the process of self-improvement, personal planning, and effective decision making. The following are important target areas for self-assessment and self-awareness because they reflect personal characteristics that play a pivotal role in promoting success in college and beyond:

- **Personal interests.** What you like to do or enjoy doing;
- **Personal values.** What is important to you and what you care about doing;
- **Personal abilities or aptitudes.** What you do well or have the potential to do well;

- **Learning habits.** How you go about learning and the usual approaches, methods, or techniques you use to learn;
- **Learning styles.** How you prefer to learn; that is, the way you like to:
  - Receive information—which learning format you prefer (e.g., reading, listening, or experiencing);
  - Perceive information—which sensory modality you prefer (e.g., vision, sound, or touch);
  - Process information—how you mentally deal with information once you have taken it in (e.g., think about it on your own or discuss it with others).
- **Personality traits.** Your temperament, emotional characteristics, and social tendencies (e.g., whether you lean toward being outgoing or reserved);
- **Academic self-concept.** What kind of student you think you are and how you perceive yourself as a learner (e.g., your level of self-confidence and whether you believe success is within your control or depends on factors beyond your control).

Self-Monitoring

Research indicates that one characteristic of successful learners is that they monitor or watch themselves and maintain self-awareness of:

- Whether they are using effective learning strategies (e.g., they are aware of their level of attention or concentration in class);
- Whether they are comprehending what they are attempting to learn (e.g., they're understanding it at a deep level or merely memorizing it at a surface level); and
- How to regulate or adjust their learning strategies to meet the demands of different tasks or subjects (e.g., they read technical material in a science textbook more slowly and stop to test their understanding more often thanwhen they're reading a novel; Pintrich, 1995; Weinstein, 1994; Weinstein & Meyer, 1991).

> "Successful students know a lot about themselves."
>
> —Claire Weinstein and Debra Meyer, professors of educational psychology at the University of Texas

Remember

Successful students are self-aware learners who know their learning strategies, styles, strengths, and shortcomings.

You can begin to establish good self-monitoring habits by getting in the routine of periodically pausing to reflect on how you're going about learning and how you're "doing" college. For instance, consider these questions:

- Am I listening attentively to what my instructor is saying in class?
- Do I comprehend what I am reading outside of class?
- Am I effectively using campus resources that are designed to support my success?

- Am I interacting with campus professionals who can contribute to my current success and future development?
- Am I interacting and collaborating with peers who can contribute to my learning and increase my level of involvement in the college experience?
- Am I effectively implementing the success strategies identified in this book?

SUMMARY AND CONCLUSION

Research reviewed in this chapter points to the conclusion that successful students are:

1. **Involved.** They invest time and effort in the college experience;

2. **Resourceful.** They capitalize on their surrounding resources;

3. **Interactive.** They interact and collaborate with others; and

4. **Reflective.** They are self-aware learners who assess and monitor their own performance.

> ### Pause for Reflection
>
> How would you rate your academic self-confidence at this point in your college experience? (Circle one.)
>
> very confident   somewhat confident
> somewhat unconfident   very unconfident
>
> Why?

Successful students are students who could honestly check almost every box in the following self-assessment checklist of success-promoting principles and practices.

A Checklist of Success-Promoting Principles and Practices

1. **Active Involvement**

   Inside the classroom:
   - **Get to class.** Treat it like a job; if you cut, your pay (grade) will be cut.
   - **Get involved in class.** Come prepared, listen actively, take notes, and participate.

   Outside the classroom:
   - **Read actively.** Take notes while you read to increase attention and retention.
   - **Double up.** Spend twice as much time on academic work outside the classroom than you spend in class—if you're a full-time student, that makes it a 40-hour academic workweek (with occasional "overtime").

2. **Use of Campus Resources**

   Capitalize on academic and student support services:
   - Learning Center

- Writing Center
- Disability Services
- College library
- Academic Advisement Center
- Office of Student Life
- Financial Aid Office
- Counseling Center
- Health Center
- Career Development Center
- Experiential Learning Resources

3. **Interpersonal Interaction and Collaboration**

    Interact with the following people:

    - **Peers.** Join student clubs and participate in campus organizations.
    - **Faculty members.** Connect with professors and other faculty members immediately after class, in their offices, or via e-mail.
    - **Academic advisors.** See an advisor for more than just a signature to register; find an advisor you can relate to and with whom you can develop an ongoing relationship.
    - **Mentors.** Try to find experienced people on campus who can serve as trusted guides and role models.

    Collaborate by doing the following:

    - **Form learning teams.** Join not only last-minute study groups but also teams that collaborate more regularly to work on such tasks as taking lecture notes, completing reading and writing assignments, conducting library research, and reviewing results of exams or course assignments.
    - **Participate in learning communities.** Enroll in two or more classes with the same students during the same term.

4. **Personal Reflection and Self-Awareness**

    - **Self-Assessment.** Reflect on and evaluate your personal traits, habits, strengths and weaknesses.
    - **Self-Monitoring.** Maintain self-awareness of how you're learning, what you're learning, and whether you're learning.

LEARNING MORE THROUGH THE WORLD WIDE WEB

Internet-Based Resources for Further Information on Liberal Arts Education

For additional information related to the ideas discussed in this chapter, we recommend the following Web sites:

Learning Strategies: www.dartmouth.edu/~acskills/success/index.html

Academic Success Strategies: www.uni.edu/walsh/linda7.html

www.lifehack.org/articles/lifehack/from-a-freshman-five-tips-for-success-in-college.html

---

Pause for Reflection

Before exiting this chapter, look back at the Checklist of Success-Promoting Principles and Practices and see how these ideas compare with those you recorded at the start of this chapter, when we asked you how you thought college would be different from high school and what it would take to be successful in college.

What ideas from your list and our checklist tend to match?

Were there any ideas on your list that were not on ours, or vice versa?

EXERCISE 1. CONSTRUCTING A MASTER LIST OF CAMPUS RESOURCES

1. Use each of the following sources to gain more in-depth knowledge about the support services available on your campus:
   - Information published in your college catalog and student handbook
   - Information posted on your college's Web site
   - Information gathered by speaking with a professional in different offices or centers on your campus

2. Using the preceding sources of information, construct a master list of all support services that are available to you on your campus. Your final product should be a list that includes the following:
   - The names of different support services your campus offers
   - The types of support each service provides
   - A short statement indicating whether you think you would benefit from each particular type of support
   - The name of a person whom you could contact for support from each service

Notes

- You can pair up with a classmate to work collaboratively on this assignment. Working together with a peer on any research task can reduce your anxiety, increase your energy, and generate synergy—which results in a final product that is superior to what could have been produced by one person working alone (independently).

- After you complete this assignment, save your master list of support services for future use. You might not have an immediate need for some of these services during your first term in college, but all of them are likely to be useful to you at some point in your college experience.

EXERCISE 2. SUPPORT SERVICES

Learning Center

Types of Support

_____

Will I benefit?   Contact Person:

_____

Will I benefit?   Contact Person:

_____

Will I benefit?   Contact Person:

Writing Center

Types of Support

_____

Will I benefit?   Contact Person:

_____

Will I benefit?   Contact Person:

_____

Will I benefit?   Contact Person:

Disability Services

Types of Support

_____

Will I benefit?   Contact Person:

_____

Will I benefit?   Contact Person:

_____

Will I benefit?   Contact Person:

College Library
Types of Support

Will I benefit?   Contact Person:

Will I benefit?   Contact Person:

Will I benefit?   Contact Person:

Academic Advisement Center
Types of Support

Will I benefit?   Contact Person:

Will I benefit?   Contact Person:

Will I benefit?   Contact Person:

Office Of Student Life
Types of Support

Will I benefit?   Contact Person:

Will I benefit?   Contact Person:

Will I benefit?   Contact Person:

NAME: _____ **DATE:** _____

Financial Aid Office

Types of Support

Will I benefit?   Contact Person:

Will I benefit?   Contact Person:

Will I benefit?   Contact Person:

Counseling Center

Types of Support

Will I benefit?   Contact Person:

Will I benefit?   Contact Person:

Will I benefit?   Contact Person:

Health Center

Types of Support

Will I benefit?   Contact Person:

Will I benefit?   Contact Person:

Will I benefit?   Contact Person:

Career Development Center

Types of Support

_____

Will I benefit?   Contact Person:

_____

Will I benefit?   Contact Person:

_____

Will I benefit?   Contact Person:

Experiential Learning Resources

Types of Support

_____

Will I benefit?   Contact Person:

_____

Will I benefit?   Contact Person:

_____

Will I benefit?   Contact Person:

Other

Types of Support

_____

Will I benefit?   Contact Person:

_____

Will I benefit?   Contact Person:

_____

Will I benefit?   Contact Person:

CASE STUDY
Alone and Disconnected: Feeling Like Calling It Quits

Josephine is a first-year student in her second week of college. She doesn't feel like she's fitting in with other students on her campus. She also feels guilty about the time she's taking time away from her family and her old high school friends who are not attending college, and she fears that her ties with them will be weakened or broken if she continues spending so much time at school and on schoolwork. Josephine is feeling so torn between college and her family and old friends that she's beginning to have second thoughts about whether she should have gone to college.

Reflection and Discussion Questions

1.   What would you say to Josephine that might persuade her to stay in college?

2.   Could the college have done more during her first 2 weeks on campus to make Josephine (and other students) feel more connected with college and less disconnected from family?

3.   Do you see anything that Josephine could do now to minimize the conflict she's experiencing between her commitment to college and her commitment to family and old friends?

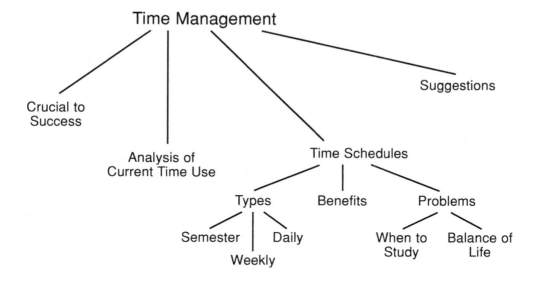

Chapter 2

Taming Time

It's a sad but true fact that much of your success or failure in college (and probably the factor that you can control the most) depends directly on how you manage your time. Even though it is such an important factor to master, it is probable that most of us have developed our "time management plan" simply by habit and not by devising a workable action plan. Have you ever stopped to consider that time is one thing in life that can never be saved? It can only be spent, and unfortunately, too many of us have developed the skill of wasting time to a fine art! We may value many things and possessions in life, yet if we had all the money in the world we could not buy one hour. Maybe we should examine this valuable commodity a little more closely!

WHY IS TIME MANAGEMENT SO CRUCIAL?

In high school, it was quite possible to waste fairly large amounts of time without dire consequences. Teachers and parents seemed to give you the benefit of the doubt and understand that you needed some leeway in your time. Even if you've been away from school, you've probably avoided assignments with due dates. But in college, your responsibilities seem to be multiplying in and out of the classroom, and the same habits of "time-waste" will soon catch up with you—possibly with unpleasant results! Many students learn this sad fact too late. Four of the major reasons for dropping out of college have been listed as economic reasons, personal reasons, academic reasons, and lack of organization skills, according to Diana Scharf Hunt—co-author of *Studying Smart: Time Management for College Students*. This lack of organization coupled with a tougher academic load means that time management suddenly becomes (or should become!) a high priority for college students if they are going to be one of the survivors. And that's not even taking into consideration that most college students want to spend some of their time participating in the vast amount of social life available or hold jobs.

Consider the possibility that all of these potential problems can be removed or prevented by the simple realization and acceptance that we frustrate ourselves by trying to control what we can't, and failing to control what we can. Time is the one thing we can never increase. But we can certainly increase our management of it by devising a plan—a workable, personalized, motivating, structuring plan.

WHAT'S THE MOST IMPORTANT THING TO LEARN IN COLLEGE?

Nothing else will be learned unless you learn to control your management of the time available to you. You either control time, or it (or the lack of it) controls you. You must decide. We all have 24 hours in a day—86,400 seconds—to fill up. How do you fill up yours?

Activity

Take a minute or two to begin filling in "The Week that Was" time schedule. Record what you have accomplished so far today. List your classes, sleeping and eating time, visiting time, dressing time, work time, and, oh yes, your study time! What if this pattern continues for the rest of the week? Continue to record what you do for one week as accurately as possible. Have you controlled time, or did it manipulate you? After you have completed the worksheet, fill in the final portion by analyzing the hours you have spent the past week doing the major necessities of college life—classes, studying, sleeping, eating, and working. Subtract your total from the total amount of hours available in a week, and then divide that by seven to get a daily amount. You may be amazed at the amount of time you waste, or at least fill up with a multitude of things that are not very important.

WHERE DID IT GO?

In a recent study at Southwest Missouri State University, students analyzed their time with these shocking results:

Time spent weekly in class—13 hours
Time spent studying—15 hours
Time spent sleeping—45 hours
Time spent eating—11 hours

Work hours (if they had jobs)—16 hours
Total hours used up—84–100 hours (depending on whether they had a job)
Total hours in a week—168 hours
*Total hours unaccounted for—68–84 hours

That's from 10–14 hours a day! Where does all of that time go? Of course, outside jobs take up some time, and errands, and visiting, and family obligations, etc. . . . But do you have 10 hours today with nothing specific to do? Of course not! No one has that kind of free time-or do they? Is it possible that it's there, and we just can't see it?

For example, did you know that the average American spends seven hours a day watching TV? Even if we said that estimate was much too high and lowered it to 25 hours of TV viewing weekly, that would be 10 years of the average 70-year life-[1/7] of your life in front of a machine! Yet in this same study, the average American only spent 19 minutes daily in active conversation, 13 minutes in hobbies, five minutes in enjoying sports, and four minutes daily in book-reading. These statistics would seem to point to the fact that Americans value TV viewing above all other pastimes, but the study concluded by the participants expressing that they value the other possibilities much more highly than TV. Maybe lack of time is not the problem; maybe it's lack of direction and planning!

The haphazard and careless use of time does at first seem to be much easier and less complicated, but it returns very poor investment dividends. Being organized and controlling your time is much easier in the long run, and less stressful! Remember the value of working smarter, not harder.

OKAY, HOW DO YOU CONTROL TIME?

There are three easy steps in learning to control your time. First, you must have a goal, or you have no purpose to plan. We have discussed the vital importance of goals earlier in this book, but keep in mind that without a goal, you will not know when you have arrived! Secondly, you must formulate a plan to reach that goal—a step-by-step way to get where you want to go. Finally, you must attack your plan and take action. Unfortunately, that's where most of our plans go awry. This is the hardest part, to just get started. We can usually finish if we can just get started! Thomas Huxley once said, "Perhaps the most valuable result of all education is the ability to make yourself do the thing you have to do, when it ought to be done, whether you like it or not." To control time you must take charge of your time by planning your priorities and devising a way to deal with them—one step at a time.

The only way you will ever be able to gain control of your busy schedule is by learning two very simple guidelines.

1.   You must learn to do your jobs as efficiently as possible so that they take the least amount of time and still produce the quality of work desired.
2.   You must learn to use the small blocks of time usually wasted.

Efficiency experts are frequently hired by large corporations to teach their workers how to produce the most in the least amount of time. Studying should be approached no differently. There are many ways to study more efficiently. Future chapters will provide you some of these ways. As for the second guideline, this is where the 10–14 "lost" hours go for most people—hidden in 18 minute, 10 minute, and four minute intervals. We conveniently convince ourselves that we cannot start, work on, or finish a job now, because we "don't have time." Most projects for busy, productive people cannot be started and finished in one neat, tidy package. It takes distributing the work load in order to finish the task. And that's why you need a time schedule!

WHAT'S THE BENEFIT OF A TIME SCHEDULE?

We'll give you several!

1. *A time schedule saves time.* It takes time to devise a schedule, but it saves time in the long run. This works in much the same way that following a map saves time when traveling. Now you can get from here to there without a map, but it's much more efficient and less stressful to decide on the best route and then follow it!

2. *A time schedule will separate work and play.* It will not rigidly control your life as you may fear, but scheduling will help provide order and discipline. This will free you to work when you work and play when you play. One of the most stressful aspects of college life is that the work never seems to be done. As one chapter is completed, another is assigned. What's the advantage of taking a test when you just have to start studying for another? If you are going to enjoy your college career and also be successful at it, you must learn to separate work and play. If you don't, your work will not be as efficient as it should be and your play will not be as enjoyable as it could be!

3. *Time schedules reduce the amount of time wasted.* Whether you choose to waste it or not, time has a way of evaporating quickly! For example, did you know that you will spend six months of your life waiting at stop signs? How do you feel about spending eight months of your life opening junk mail, or one whole year looking for lost items? And then there are those five years of waiting in line. If you are going to waste time, you should do the deciding about when to waste it!

4. *Scheduling time helps to decrease your "slacking off" periods.* Most humans tend to slack off in their work habits and productivity near the end of the day, the week, the semester, and so forth. If you plan your schedule you can help to prevent this, or even accommodate this tendency by utilizing your "prime time." This is that time when you are at your peak efficiency and when you can accomplish the most. You won't need to feel guilty about slacking off if you have already achieved your projected plan.

5. *Time schedules help prevent cramming.* If the only benefit of a time schedule was that it helped to prevent cramming and thus promote retention of learning, we feel it would be worth it! Research after research proves the benefit of distributing your study times into several periods rather than one massive period of torture the night before the test or assignment. Not only will you remember more with this spacing out of studying, but your health and emotional well-being will have a better chance to prosper. Physically as well as academically, cramming does not pay! Just as a path in the woods is more easily seen if traveled over several times, material is more easily recalled if rehearsed at different sessions.

6. *A time schedule helps to promote balance in your life*-a balance of work, study, recreation, and free time. You need breaks as you study (10 minutes for every hour or so is a good rule of thumb), and you need recreation to re-create your body, soul, and spirit. If your balance of life gets out of whack, it is hard to enjoy any aspect of it fully.

7. *Scheduling helps daily chores get accomplished.* By planning it out, maybe you could find a way to manage those chores that seem to get out of hand so easily—things like getting the dishes or the laundry done, writing to your family, or even paying the bills. Schedule a time when you will take care of these little-but-necessary jobs, and half the work is done.

8. *Are you too busy?* One of the greatest benefits of a schedule may be to find out if you CAN get all this stuff done! You may be asking too much of yourself. It simply may not be realistic to work 32 hours a week and take 19 credit hours, plus raise two children (or find time for two boyfriends—whichever fits your situation)! You may find that you must drop certain activities, combine projects, reduce the frequency of events, or alternate weeks in order to live sanely.

9. *Time schedules help you to overcome the worst hurdle of all-getting started!* We tend to avoid the doing of disliked tasks, or substitute doing jobs that are less important, but more appealing. We procrastinate to the best of our ability if it suits our purpose or mood for the moment.

THE PROBLEM WITH PROCRASTINATION

If we could learn to solve this problem, most of our time worries would be solved. For most college students, procrastination is the worst academic problem they face, except for the problem of remembering what they have learned. Procrastination seems to be the main cause of anxiety and worry in the overall picture—we could have done a better job and been less stressed out if we just had more time to do the job! And we could have had more time if we had started the job before the last minute. Procrastination means needlessly postponing tasks until later, and it is really just a strategy that people use to protect themselves from certain fears. These fears usually involve the fear of failing, or even succeeding! Statements like: "I must be perfect," "It's safer to do nothing than do the wrong thing," or "If I do a good job, I may have to do an even better job next time" are common thoughts for procrastinators. Many of us probably fall into this category if we are honest with ourselves. Overcoming procrastination is a matter of habit and will-power, and the only way to cure the problem is to face the fears. Setting daily goals, prioritizing, breaking the job into small, easily-accomplished sub-parts, setting time limits, and rewarding yourself for an accomplished task may help you with the procrastination problem.

HOW DO YOU MAKE A TIME SCHEDULE?

You will first need to consider what type of time schedule or schedules will best suit your purposes. There are daily schedules, weekly schedules, or semester schedules, and you may need one or all of these. As a suggested minimum, you will need a semester calendar, an average weekly master plan, and a daily list. If you want the maximum of efficiency, you need to incorporate all three types of schedules.

The Semester Calendar

As soon as you get your different class syllabi for a new semester, you should fill out as much of a semester calendar as you can. Plot test dates, due dates, (VACATION DATES!), and begin to develop an overall scheme of busy weeks versus planning weeks. You might even plot in notes to yourself like "Start worrying about term paper topic" or "Two tests coming up in two weeks" on your calendar at the appropriate locations. You will begin to feel a little more in control as soon as your calendar is in shape. Now all you have to do is plan on how to accomplish the week-by-week tasks.

The Weekly Master Plan

Let's now work on making a weekly schedule for an average week in your current semester. On the Master Time Schedule provided, you should first schedule in the names of the classes you are taking. Attending class may not be your only "job" right now, but it should certainly be a very high priority if you are going to be successful in college. In a very real aspect, attending class is your career right now. Do it professionally!

Secondly, go back through the time schedule and list those demands on your time that do not vary that much from week to week. You might call this "Necessary Time." It would include such things as outside jobs, eating, sleeping, clubs, sports, practices, commuting time, church, housekeeping chores, etc.

After having filled in CLASS TIME and NECESSARY TIME, you are now ready to figure out STUDY TIME. In order to accomplish this task, you should first analyze your study time from "The Week That Was" Time Schedule you filled out. Take a minute to complete the Time Analyzer Worksheet before you go any further and then decide how you measure up. You should try to remediate problems that you are giving yourself by your study behavior. Remember, your goal is to study smarter, not harder. The step of deciding WHAT to study WHEN will be one of the most important decisions you will make this semester. We'll look at this carefully in the next section.

Finally, the blank spaces that will remain in your time schedule after you fill in your study time will be your FREE TIME. We usually can find plenty of ways to fill in these blanks as the days go by. We've provided you with an extra copy of a Master Schedule so you can make more copies as the need arises. Use it! The problem that must now be dealt with is how to schedule that study time.

HOW DO I DECIDE WHEN TO STUDY?

In the first place, you need to decide how much time is needed for study. In high school, 15–30 minutes per class was usually sufficient, but those days are gone! Usually a 2/1 ratio is suggested-that is, two hours of study for every hour of class time. So a very general rule would be that if you were carrying 15 credit hours, you should find 30 hours of study time. Of course, some classes might not require this, but some may require more. It is much wiser to plan too much time and not need it than to not plan enough and find out too late just how badly it was needed! Usually a one hour study session with a ten minute break could be a workable goal for most students. You would need to adapt this to what is most produc-tive for you; 30- or 45-minute slots with five minute breaks might be more beneficial.

As to how to pick the most productive time to study each subject, consider these guidelines.

1. The OPTIMUM TIME for the most efficiency is usually RIGHT AFTER THE CLASS. To study the subject right BEFORE THE CLASS meets can be very advantageous for discussion classes, or even just a quick review of notes before a lecture can make those classes more beneficial. To pick a time slot right after class can increase your efficiency and decrease the time needed to study. For example, a 30-minute study immediately after class could be worth one hour of study later. You tend to be more interested in the subject at that time, need less warm-up time to get involved in the studying, and there tends to be less confusion about assignments if they are started quickly.

2. Try planning a time to REVIEW your notes immediately BEFORE YOU GO TO SLEEP. Plan on learning new material when you are fresh, but review right before you retire. Studies have shown that you retain this reviewed material better if you sleep on it. In fact, the shorter the delay between study and bed, the more likely you are to retain the material!

3. Plan on studying your MOST DIFFICULT CLASSES IN THE EARLY AFTERNOON, for the most part. Long-term memory seems to be more effective then, as well as hand-eye coordination and physical strength. If you need to memorize or juggle words or figures, your short-term memory is more effective in the morning, so plan those types of activities for earlier hours. Beware of general low-energy time zones-for most people these center around 2–5 p.m. (when neural functions decline and blood sugar levels are lower) or 2–7 a.m. (when most accidents that can be attributed to human error occur). These might not be the optimum times to write that difficult research paper.

4. FOLLOW YOUR BIOLOGICAL CLOCK. Find your prime times and work with your body rather than fighting against its natural tendencies. To find whether you are a night person (an owl) or a morning person (a lark), take the inventory and then plan to study for tests at your peak periods. Morning people tend to jump out of bed early in the morning with a drive to have a productive morning. They tend to lead controlled, structured, well-regulated lives. They begin to slow down about mid-afternoon and believe and follow the old adage of "Early to bed, early to rise . . ."

   On the other hand, night people (or owls) crawl rather than jump out of bed, barely survive mornings, begin to wake up about noon and become their normally extroverted selves, peak in mid-afternoon, and wind down quite a bit later. No one tendency is the correct one, but you must work with your preference or it will defeat you. Don't plan on getting up early and cramming for the big final if you are a night owl. You probably won't make it up! And if you are a morning lark, you'd better not go ahead and attend the big party with lofty plans to study all night long. Your body won't make things easy for you to follow through with your plans. Consider these factors when you schedule classes.

   One final thought about your body's biological clock is that most people tend to find benefit in keeping in step with the sun. There seems to be some added benefits to working during daylight hours and resting during night hours.

5. Make sure you SPACE YOUR STUDYING PROPERLY. Remember to plan and use breaks that vary greatly from what your study activity was. Alternate different types of study activities. For example, plan to study an activity subject (such as math or composition) between subjects that require a lot of reading. And make sure you space out the studying required for each subject. It will usually be more effective to study biology in three one-half hour sessions rather than one and one-half hour session. Don't forget to include a time to review past notes also. Otherwise, you will be practically starting over when it is time for testing.

6. DOUBLE TIME ESTIMATES AS YOU PLAN. Things always seem to take longer than originally thought. In fact, you need to guard against "Parkinson's Law"— work always stretches to fill whatever time is available. Instead of planning on studying one hour, plan how much you will get accomplished in one hour. Set goals and limits and you will be able to achieve more.

7. Plan to STUDY EACH SUBJECT AT THE SAME TIME, ON THE SAME DAYS, AND IN THE SAME PLACE (one place with everything you need close at hand). Again, the idea is to work with your body instead of against it, and you can condition your body to not resist studying so much if you establish very firm habits. If you have psychology on Mondays, Wednesdays, and Fridays, the best time to study would be on those days at whatever time you designate would fit your biological clock, your time schedule, and be closest to psychology class time.

8. In general, plan to study the WORST FIRST, EASIEST (OR MORE INTERESTING) LAST. Prioritize, and then plan on getting the tough stuff over while your energy and initiative are at their peaks.

WHAT ABOUT "DAILY" TIME MANAGEMENT?

As you try to follow your weekly Master Time Schedule, you will also need to make daily plans. A good suggestion is to make out this daily plan before you go to bed at night. Although it takes time and energy, devising a list of what you would like to accomplish the next day will help give you direction and purpose, and start your day more efficiently. But one more step is needed—prioritize that list before you start sawing logs. That way if you don't get everything done you will at least have accomplished the most important things. Try making some copies of the Daily Plan Worksheet we've provided, and see if it doesn't help you to put life into perspective and order. You're beginning to get a grip on it!

ANY OTHER TIME MANAGEMENT TIPS?

Sure! Take a look at these:

1. Make studying as portable as possible. Carry pocket work/note cards to study when you are on the go.

2. Use those small blocks of time usually wasted. Recite, review, and plan in-between classes, while waiting in lines, etc. Carry a small notepad to help you plan.

3. Make lists and prioritize them. This idea paid one man (efficiency expert Ivy Lee) $25,000 and made Bethlehem Steel Company and Charles Schwab, its president, a

CRITICAL THINKING

Take a minute to look back on yesterday's events. Write down all the things that you did yesterday—in the order that you did them. Analyze your accomplishments. Did you think about the priority of the task as you started to work? Did you really accomplish the things that needed to be taken care of yesterday? Would there have been a better order to have worked on those tasks, or should some tasks have been omitted and others substituted? Try prioritizing yesterday's events now in the light of a new day. If you had worked in this order yesterday, would today's tasks be any easier or more organized? Keep this activity in mind as you think about whether to make a list and prioritize it for tomorrow!

hundred million dollars! Lee instructed each steel worker to make a list each day, prioritize the list, and then work on the first item until it was done. Then, and only then, they were to move on to the second item. This strategy turned that little known company into the biggest independent steel producer in the world. The idea was simple then, and is still simply effective now—take things one at a time in their proper order.

4. Recognize four things that will steal more time from you than you can make up for—laziness, sidetracks, procrastination, and day-dreaming. These things must constantly be fought.

5. Use calendars, clocks, appointment books, and notepads to their full advantage by planning ahead, organizing, and following the plan.

6. Try to handle each task only once. Finish the job as much as your schedule will allow before proceeding to the next task.

7. Practice trading time, not stealing it. Has an unexpected social event popped up? Go ahead and attend guilt-free-as long as you trade the study time you had planned for free time later in your schedule. Don't just put it off-plan and trade it.

8. Learn to say no, and mean it.

9. Control interruptions.

10. Avoid perfectionism. Shoot for your best, but don't overdo this time-sapper.

11. Plan, and then start! Remember: the more time spent planning, the less time needed to accomplish the task. When it's time to start the task, throw yourself into it with enthusiasm. Don't wait for inspiration to strike. It probably won't. Don't inch into the water—dive in! Genuine enthusiasm may follow!

MASTERING THE TIME TRAP

Now that you know why to do it, and how to do it, let's do it! Devise your master time schedule and diligently attempt to follow it. You may soon find that there are a lot of benefits in being the master OF—rather than being mastered BY—your time. You can win in the game of time if you learn what the worn-out, frustrated student in this example learned:

> *"I can't keep our appointment," he sighed. "I find myself swamped. It's getting to be too much!"*
>
> *"You've contracted a malady about as unique as the common cold," replied his friend. "It's called Wrong Ending. You know, we were all given two ends to use. On one we sit, with one we muse. Success depends on which we use . . . heads you win, tails you lose."*

One final comment-don't forget the importance of balance in your life. Does your time schedule have a balance of work and play, study and recreation? Get your life too much out of balance in either direction and you are asking for trouble. You're on your way to a bright future if you learn the secret of mastering your time! And what a secret to learn, for the waste of time is one price winners can't afford to pay!

SUMMARY

In this chapter we have discussed the fact that it is critical to master time management in college in order to succeed academically AND socially. College students are very busy people with places to go, family obligations, people to see, and tests for which to study! None of these things can happen efficiently unless one learns to control the balance of work and play in his life. Effective people must also learn to work out a manageable way to arrange their schedule so that they are making the best use of the time they have. Lack of time is really not the problem; procrastination and poor planning are the real culprits. We learn to control time by devising and learning to follow a time schedule that takes into consideration our schedules, goals, priorities, and biological make-up. The benefits of this planning device are numerous, including distributing the work load and helping to reduce stress. This chapter has given you an opportunity to make a time schedule and suggestions for choosing your optimum study times. There are ways to make time management more efficient and effective, and the suggestions included in the last section of the chapter should give you some positive steps to take in the right direction!

NAME: _____ **DATE:** _____

"THE WEEK THAT WAS" YOUR CURRENT TIME SCHEDULE

	MONDAY	TUESDAY	WEDNESDAY	THURSDAY	FRIDAY	SATURDAY	SUNDAY
6:00 a.m.							
7:00 a.m.							
8:00 a.m.							
9:00 a.m.							
10:00 a.m.							
11:00 a.m.							
noon							
1:00 p.m.							
2:00 p.m.							
3:00 p.m.							
4:00 p.m.							
5:00 p.m.							
6:00 p.m.							
7:00 p.m.							
8:00 p.m.							
9:00 p.m.							
10:00 p.m.							
11:00 p.m.							
midnight							
1:00 a.m.							
2:00 a.m.							

Totals:

Hours Spent in Class	_____	168	(total hours in 1 week)
Hours Spent Studying	_____ – _____		(your total of "necessary hours")
Hours Spent Sleeping	_____ _____		(hours unaccounted for weekly)
Hours Spent Eating	_____		
Hours Spent Working	========	7⌐̄ ̄ ̄ ̄	(hours unaccounted for PER DAY!)
Total	_____		

44

TIME ANALYZER FOR "THE WEEK THAT WAS" WORKSHEET

Analyze your current time usage by answering these questions based on what is normal for you.

		YES	NO
1.	I often study at a time when I am not at peak efficiency due to fatigue.	_____	_____
2.	I have failed to complete at least one assignment on time this semester.	_____	_____
3.	This week I spent time watching TV, visiting, or napping that really should have been spent otherwise.	_____	_____
4.	Often, lack of prioritizing tasks causes me some difficulty in completing tasks on time.	_____	_____
5.	Social or athletic events cause me to neglect academic work fairly often.	_____	_____
6.	At least once this semester, I have not remembered that an assignment was due until the night before.	_____	_____
7.	I often get behind in one course due to having to work on another.	_____	_____
8.	I usually wait until the night before the due date to start assignments	_____	_____
9.	My studying is often a hit-or-miss strategy which is dependent on my mood.	_____	_____
10.	I normally wait until test time to read texts and/or review lecture notes.	_____	_____
11.	I often have the sinking realization that there is simply not enough time left to accomplish the assignment or study sufficiently for the test.	_____	_____
12.	Often I rationalize that very few people will make the A/get the project done on time/really read the text, etc.	_____	_____
13.	I catch myself looking forward to study interruptions rather than trying to avoid them.	_____	_____
14.	I have failed to eliminate some time wasters this past week that I could have controlled.	_____	_____
15.	I often feel out of control in respect to time.	_____	_____
16.	I have procrastinated at least twice this week.	_____	_____
17.	I find myself doing easier or more interesting tasks first, even if they are not as important.	_____	_____
18.	I feel I have wasted quite a lot of time-again-this week.	_____	_____
19.	I studied EACH course I am currently taking this week.	_____	_____
20.	I spent some time this week reviewing previous weeks' notes even though I did not have a test.	_____	_____
21.	The time of day that I am the most alert is _____ , so I tried to study my hardest subjects then.	_____	_____

	YES	NO
22. I studied approximately 1–2 hours out of class for every hour in class.	———	———
23. My most sluggish period during the day is _____ , so I used these times to relax or participate in sports or hobbies.	———	———
24. I often make out daily lists of tasks to be completed, and I prioritize these lists.	———	———
25. I use small blocks of time (10–30 min.) between classes to review notes, start assignments, or plan.	———	———

To calculate your score, score 1 point for each yes from items 1–18, and 1 point for each no from items 19–25. The higher your score, the more you need a Master Time Schedule! Consider these categories for your score:

15–19 YOU'RE IN DESPERATE NEED OF A PLAN! How do you ever get anything accomplished? (Or do you?)

10–14 YOU NEED A PLAN! Life could be simpler if you took the time to plan it out.

5–9 A PLAN WOULD HELP! The going could be smoother, and more could be accomplished.

0–4 A PLAN COULDN'T HURT! You're doing pretty well, but give yourself the gift of organization, and you may give yourself the gift of more time.

Please write a paragraph that reflects on your results.

_____

_____

_____

_____

_____

_____

_____

_____

_____

_____

_____

_____

_____

_____

_____

_____

NAME: _____ DATE: _____

MASTER TIME SCHEDULE

	MONDAY	TUESDAY	WEDNESDAY	THURSDAY	FRIDAY	SATURDAY	SUNDAY
6:00 a.m.							
7:00 a.m.							
8:00 a.m.							
9:00 a.m.							
10:00 a.m.							
11:00 a.m.							
noon							
1:00 p.m.							
2:00 p.m.							
3:00 p.m.							
4:00 p.m.							
5:00 p.m.							
6:00 p.m.							
7:00 p.m.							
8:00 p.m.							
9:00 p.m.							
10:00 p.m.							
11:00 p.m.							
midnight							
1:00 a.m.							
2:00 a.m.							

NAME: _____ **DATE:** _____

MASTER TIME SCHEDULE

	MONDAY	TUESDAY	WEDNESDAY	THURSDAY	FRIDAY	SATURDAY	SUNDAY
6:00 a.m.							
7:00 a.m.							
8:00 a.m.							
9:00 a.m.							
10:00 a.m.							
11:00 a.m.							
noon							
1:00 p.m.							
2:00 p.m.							
3:00 p.m.							
4:00 p.m.							
5:00 p.m.							
6:00 p.m.							
7:00 p.m.							
8:00 p.m.							
9:00 p.m.							
10:00 p.m.							
11:00 p.m.							
midnight							
1:00 a.m.							
2:00 a.m.							

MORNING LARK VS. NIGHT OWL

This questionnaire can help you determine if you are a morning person (a lark) or a night person (an owl). "Larks" usually lead well-structured, controlled lives. They jump out of bed and usually have productive mornings, tending to wind down about mid-afternoon. "Owls," on the other hand, tend to crawl out of bed, barely live through mornings, but have more productive afternoons. They also tend to be more extroverted than larks. Which are you? Find out by circling the answer most appropriate for you and adding up your points.

		Points Possible	Points Earned
1.	I feel best if I get up around:		_____
	5–6:30 a.m.	5	
	6:30–7:30 a.m.	4	
	7:30–9:30 a.m.	3	
	9:30–11 a.m.	2	
	11–noon	1	
2.	If I had to describe how easy it is for me to get up in the morning, I would say:		_____
	It is not easy at all!	1	
	It is not very easy.	2	
	It is fairly easy.	3	
	It is very easy.	4	
3.	The way I feel for the first half-hour after I wake up is:		_____
	very tired	1	
	fairly tired	2	
	fairly refreshed	3	
	very refreshed	4	
4.	If I could choose the best time to take a difficult test, it would be:		_____
	8–10 a.m.	4	
	10 a.m.–1 p.m.	3	
	1–5 p.m.	2	
	7–9 p.m.	1	
5.	If my job would require that I work from 4–6 am one day, I would choose to:		_____
	not go to bed until after I worked	1	
	take a nap before and sleep after	2	
	sleep before work and nap after	3	
	get all the sleep I need before work	4	

	Points Possible	Points Earned

6. If someone asked me to jog with them at 7 a.m. one morning,
    I would perform: _____

	Points Possible
well	4
reasonably well	3
not very well	2
not well at all	1

7. If I have to wake up at a specific time each morning,
    I depend on my alarm clock: _____

	Points Possible
not at all	4
slightly	3
quite a lot	2
desperately	1

8. I am usually tired and wanting to go to bed by: _____

	Points Possible
8–9 p.m.	5
9–10:30 p.m.	4
10:30 p.m.–12:30 a.m.	3
12:30–2 a.m.	2
2–3 a.m.	1

TOTAL NUMBER OF POINTS EARNED

A score of 20 is halfway between owl and lark. The higher your score, the more of a morning lark you are. The lower your score, the more of a night owl you are.

NAME: _____ **DATE:** _____

DAILY PLAN FOR _____
(DATE)

JOBS TO COMPLETE	DUE DATE	PRIORITY	COMPLETED?
1.			
2.			
3.			
4.			
5.			
6.			
7.			
8.			
9.			
10.			

PHONE CALLS TO MAKE			
1.			
2.			
3.			
4.			

ERRANDS TO RUN	DUE DATE	PRIORITY	COMPLETED?
1.			
2.			
3.			
4.			
5.			
6.			

PEOPLE TO SEE			
1.			
2.			
3.			
4.			

Notes to Myself

_____

_____

_____

_____

_____

_____

_____

_____

_____

_____

_____

_____

_____

_____

_____

_____

_____

_____

_____

_____

_____

_____

_____

Chapter 3

Learning Style
One's Distinctive Manner of Learning

Learning is an individual, creative process. Each person has a preferred way of doing things, a unique approach to gathering, assimilating, and retaining information. This approach is called your learning style and reflects your individual pattern of thinking and learning. You have an incredible capacity to learn. Do you take advantage of this innate ability? When you have information to process and learn, do you challenge your mind by utilizing the most effective and efficient learning strategies compatible with your particular pattern of learning?

In this chapter, we will explore how to use your learning strengths and how differences in personality, perceptual learning modalities, life experiences, environmental factors, and brain dominance influence the way we think and learn. There are several assessments in this chapter that can help you identify your personal learning style, or the various learning patterns that you engage in to think, recall, create, and solve problems.

WHOLE-BRAIN LEARNING

Did you know that most people lose around 90% of what they read and hear within 24 hours of being exposed to new information unless the information is organized and reviewed? Becoming more knowledgeable about how you personally use your brain to think increases the probability of developing more effective learning patterns and strategies for comprehension and retention.

The average brain weighs about 2–3 pounds and serves as the command center for interpreting sensory input, coordinating bodily activities, and processing emotions and cognition. Most of the cranial cavity is occupied by the cerebrum, which is divided into two cerebral hemispheres, a right hemisphere and a left hemisphere. A large nerve track called the corpus callosum joins the right and left hemispheres and carries messages back and forth between the two sides, allowing them to exchange information.

The neurosurgeon Roger Sperry (1974) did research on the brain to prove that the two hemispheres of the brain process information differently (split-brain theory). He was awarded a Noble Prize for his efforts. His research was based on subjects who had experienced severe epileptic seizures and opted for surgery to have their corpus callosum severed to control the seizures. The two hemispheres of the brain then could no longer communicate with one another. Because the right brain, which governs visual memory and spatial reasoning, controls the left side of the body and the left brain, which handles language and speech, controls the right side of the body, Sperry's subjects forgot how to draw with their right hand and how to write with their left hand. The neurologist Oliver Sacks (1970) reported that he once worked with a well-known musician and teacher who was capable of recognizing prominent features and other details around him but unable to grasp the whole picture due to damage to the right side of his brain. He suffered from what is called visual agnosia. He would walk down the street, "magoo-like," patting the tops of water hydrants and parking meters, mistakenly thinking they were children. Once when leaving Dr. Sacks's office, the client reached for his hat and instead took hold of his wife's head. The incident became the title of his book *The Man Who Mistook His Wife for a Hat.*

People characteristically display a predominant hemispherical preference. In other words, you tend to use one side of your brain more than the other. Our problem-solving skills, mental and physical abilities, and even our personality traits are influenced by the way in which we use the right and left sides of our brain (Wonder & Donovan, 1984).

Right-Brain

The right brain thinks holistically and intuitively, unable to process language. Mental processes associated with the right brain register in our consciousness as feelings and hunches, based on visual-spatial reasoning (e.g., recognition of patterns including faces, drawing, dancing, and other movements). Information is often processed visually (and spatially), kinesthetically (through movement), and haptically (through touch). The right brain excels in abstract thinking and prefers to synthesize rather than analyze information, merging patterns of related information together to form "the big picture." It is because of the right brain that we can make sense out of maps, recognize faces, and perceive our emotions. General overviews at the beginning of a chapter in a textbook can prove especially helpful to a right-brain dominant learner. If you are using the right brain for problem solving, try following your hunches, daydream, brainstorm, and take long walks to mull over your ideas.

Left-Brain

The left brain thinks analytically and reductively by breaking information into parts and processing the information sequentially. The left brain helps us to make logical sense out of experience. Mental processes associated with the left brain include language (e.g., speech, written language, verbal memory, and reading) and mathematics. Unlike the right brain, which prefers to concentrate on a variety of issues and views, the left brain prefers to concentrate on just a single issue or point of view and look at the pros and cons of that view.

The lists below summarize some of the main traits of right-brain and left-brain thinking. Which best describes the way you think?

Left-Brain	**Right-Brain**
Analytical, linear thinking	Holistic, intuitive thinking
Sequential, orderly	Looks for patterns and relationships

Language	Nonverbal
Mathematics	Synthesizes information
Singular focus	Focuses on a variety of things
Concrete, responds to facts	Abstract, responds to theories
Labels things	Refers to things

When we speak about left brain and right brain, we are referring to different types of information processing, but the two distinct hemispheres are connected and communicate with one another. The right half and the left half of the cerebrum function as a whole, each hemisphere contributing a portion of the experience. No one can totally turn off or turn on either side of the brain. You can increase your potential to learn by using a diversity of learning strategies that pull from both parts of the brain. Whether people are predominantly right brain or left brain, when mental areas of the brain once considered weak are further developed, a synergetic effect occurs in which all areas of mental performance improve (Buzan, 1976).

What can you do to better develop a whole-brain approach to learning? In class while listening to lectures, you can remind yourself to shift your body position, pay careful attention to the speaker's body language, outline your notes, listen for facts, and notice any patterns of information that emerge from the lecture. Above all, listen with an intent to learn. Always assume that you will learn something from whatever you are engaged in. Learn to shift back and forth between right brain and left brain whenever the style you are engaging in (right-brain or left-brain) is not working for you. For example, if you are right-brain dominant and are working a math problem, you might see the solution but not the sequential steps to the solution. If you are only given credit if you show the steps, then there may be a problem. Consider another example. You are completing a history exam, and you have been asked to trace the key events that led up to the Voting Rights Act of 1965. Thinking from the right side of your brain, you might remember the events leading up to the Voting Act and understand the relationship among them but not be able to recall significant dates, names, and pertinent legislation. In both situations, engaging the left brain more would help.

On the other hand, suppose you are left-brain dominant and are working a math problem. You might remember the steps, but no matter how hard you try to solve the problem using the steps presented in class to a similar problem, you cannot arrive at the correct answer. You are probably having difficulty understanding the theory involved and seeing the overall pattern. Consider the history test example. This time, you can remember all the dates and the names of key figures but not the overall pattern of events. Engaging the right side of your brain would help with both situations.

How do you jump back and forth from the right to the left and from the left to the right? You do this continually throughout the day as you make sense of the world around you. But if you are predominantly thinking from the right side and need to get the left side more engaged, start doing multiplication tables or figure out how much time you have left to complete the test. If you are processing information predominantly from the left side of the brain and want to move over to the right, daydream, visualize, meditate, or focus your attention on a visual point in the distance.

Most of the academic learning that occurs in colleges engages the logical, linear, orderly left brain. For students who use more of the right brain and think holistically and intuitively, learning can often be a frustrating experience. Since responsibility for learning rests with you, the student, it is essential that you become aware of your learning patterns and how to use the power of your brain more effectively for learning.

MULTIPLE INTELLIGENCES

Howard Gardner (1993), a developmental psychologist, proposes that we possess not only a multitude of talents but also "multiple intelligences." His research emerged from an inquiry on the topic of human potential in which he participated as part of a team of researchers from the Harvard Graduate School of Education. According to Gardner there are at least seven different forms of intelligence: body-kinesthetic intelligence, linguistic intelligence, spatial intelligence, interpersonal intelligence, intrapersonal intelligence, musical intelligence, and logical-mathematical intelligence. We are all intelligent in numerous ways.

- **Body-kinesthetic intelligence** relates to fine-motor and gross-motor skills. People who excel in this type of intelligence have superior eye-hand coordination, are skilled in figuring out how things work, and may excel in sports.
- **Linguistic intelligence** is an ability exhibited by linguistic processing. Creative writers, poets, public speakers, and others who are sensitive to language and meaning excel in linguistic intelligence.
- **Spatial intelligence** relates to the ability to form a mental model and then mentally manipulate the model and use it. People who have a talent for sculpting, graphic design, abstract art, and other skills associated with mental imagery are thought to have well-developed spatial intelligence.
- **Interpersonal intelligence** is the ability to understand people. Religious leaders, counselors, journalists, teachers, and other leaders often excel in this area of intelligence.
- **Intrapersonal intelligence** refers to the ability to know one's self. Self-knowledge is being aware of and able to reflect on personal motivations for behaving, thinking, and feeling.
- **Musical intelligence** is the ability to sing or play music well but also includes the ability to enjoy music and performances.
- **Logical-mathematical intelligence** relates to math and science skills. Is it easy for you to understand philosophy, math, or science courses? Do you enjoy solving problems? If so, you may excel in logical-mathematical intelligence.

Each person draws from a different combination of these seven intelligences just as we use a combination of our senses in the learning process.

PERCEPTUAL LEARNING MODALITIES

Modalities are preferred senses that one uses to gather information from the environment. Michael Galbraith and Waynne James (1985) identified seven specific perceptual modalities: print, visual, auditory, interactive, kinesthetic, haptic, and olfactory. These learning modalities are based on the five senses: seeing, hearing, touching, smelling, and tasting. Modalities that you use more effectively than others in learning are your strengths. The more modalities you use to learn, the greater your recall will likely be. For example, if you read something and then write it down or tell someone about it, you will have a better chance of recalling the information when you need it. Learn to take advantage of strong modalities and strengthen the weaker ones. You will be taking in information all around you.

Below are the descriptions of the seven perceptual learning modalities.

Print. If you retain information easily when reading, and when studying you tend to focus well on what you have read, then the print modality is a learning strength for you. Reading and writing are the primary ways that you process information. Print learners prefer written material and learn best when reading on their own. Underlining key terms and annotations written in your own words as well as summaries are good study strategies for a print learner.

Visual. When taking a test, do you ever try to remember the information from the upper right corner of your notes or from the middle of the page, or next to that fantastic doodle down the side of your notes? Chances are you are trying to locate the information visually and spatially, drawing on the visual-spatial memory center located in the right part of the brain. Visual learners learn best through observation. In conversations, a visual learner will often say "I see" or "Picture that." For a visual learner, information is best processed when reduced and displayed in a visual format such as pictures, slides, diagrams, graphs, charts, and symbols. Color is also helpful to visual learners. When given directions, visual learners prefer that they be written down rather than spoken. Maps are even better.

Interactive. Do you like study groups? When you were younger, did you get a family member or friend to review information for a test by quizzing you? Do you try to get a discussion going in class if possible? People who learn best through verbalizations, like discussions and group projects, and learn through teaching others, utilize an interactive learning modality. If interactive learners have no one to study with, they can still study interactively by making a question-and-answer study guide. They can then tape themselves reading the questions and answers. While studying, they can then play the tape, listen to the question, and then press pause. The person then has the opportunity to answer and can check the answer by releasing pause.

Auditory. When taking a test or rewriting notes, do you hear your professor's voice in your head? Does listening to audiotaped summaries of your notes and explanations of specific concepts help you learn information? Auditory learners learn best from listening to lectures, reading aloud, and other auditory stimulation.

Haptic. In biology classes if the teacher was using a model of the human skeletal structure to lecture, did you find yourself wanting to touch the model? Haptic learners learn best by doing; they prefer a hands-on approach to learning. They can benefit from building models where they manipulate objects or from using sticky notes, poster board, and magic markers. They will often take a trial-and-error approach to learning, using their hands to touch or feel. Notecards and computers can be great study aides. Haptic learners like concrete examples and often get more out of lab sessions than in-class instruction.

Kinesthetic. What are you doing when you study? Is your leg kicking back and forth? Are you moving about the room? Are you tapping or chewing on a pencil? Kinesthetic learners process information best through movement. While studying, they spend time recopying notes, writing lists, and outlining chapters. Notecards are helpful. They might separate the cards into piles, differentiating one pile from the other by how well they know the information. When writing a paper, they might write all ideas on notecards and then rearrange them as they synthesize and organize information to structure the paper. The next time you observe someone clicking his or her pencil or tapping it on the desk while thinking, realize that the person is not necessarily trying to drive you crazy. He or she may just be a kinesthetic learner using movement to retrieve information from long-term memory.

Olfactory. Did you know that olfactory learners just need to sniff their textbooks to prepare for an upcoming final? Just kidding. Some people, though, do have a strong sense of odor discrimination, so odors can affect their ability to concentrate and process information. We all associate some memories with particular smells and tastes. Students majoring in chemistry, animal science, and medicine often use their sense of smell to differentiate information. Many people use aromatherapy to relax. Could you study better in a room where scented candles were burning? Is it possible for you to study in an area that smells bad?

As a learner, you need to develop a repertoire of good study skills based on your own unique learning patterns and also learn to adapt your learning preference to the instructional style of the professor. Print and auditory learners have the best advantage in a university setting. You read, write, listen to lectures, and take notes. Interactive learners might excel in languages, whereas kinesthetic learners might do well in dance and physical education. Perceptual preferences affect success in certain academic areas. A visual learner who does not include charts, graphs, and other visual interpretations of information while learning may not learn to his or her full potential. Imagine you are a visual learner and someone gives you detailed directions to a location verbally. Will you remember the information if you cannot write it down or draw a map? The same is true for a kinesthetic or haptic learner who decides not to use notecards or similar means to study for class.

PERSONALITY

Each person is unique. Each person thinks differently, acts differently, has various wants and needs, finds different things to be sources of pleasure and frustration, and conceptualizes and understands things differently. The psychotherapist Carl Jung said that beneath the surface of all of these differences are preferences about ways of interacting with people, perceiving information in the surrounding environment, making decisions, and acting on decisions that give rise to various personality types. These different personality types influence the way you learn. Jung's theory about personality types is the basis for a personality assessment developed by Isabel Myers and Katharine Briggs named the Myers-Briggs Type Indicator (MBTI) (Myers, 1995).

The MBTI identifies 16 personality types based on individual preferences. Four dimensions differentiate personality types: introversion-extroversion, intuition-sensation, thinking-feeling, and judging-perceiving. Complete the personality assessment in Exercise 3 at the end of the chapter to discover your type. Then read through the following descriptions of the four dimensions to learn more about the influence of personality and learning.

Introversion-Extroversion

When solving a problem, do you prefer to talk with others or think it through alone? Do you tend to be more aware of what is going on around you or more aware of what you are thinking and feeling? The dimensions of introversion and extroversion are related to how people energize themselves in different situations, including learning.

Introversion (I). Introverts are reflective learners, scanning inwardly for stimulation. They become energized as they reflect and think about ideas. In an academic setting, introverts prefer working alone because they can comprehend better if they take the time to organize and think about the information before them. Introverts have a tendency not to speak up in class as all their energy is spent on thinking and reflecting about ideas. Introverts plan out thoughts and words before writing, stop frequently to think as they write, prefer quiet places to study, and dislike interruptions. They spend so much time thinking and reflecting that they may start daydreaming about how things might be, and opportunities sometimes pass them by.

Extroversion (E). Extroverts are active learners who focus their attention outwardly for stimulation. They learn new information best when they can apply it to the external world. Extroverts are energized by people and thus prefer interacting with others while learning. They tend to participate in class, enjoying group projects, discussions, and study groups (similar to the interactive learners). Extroverts tend to jump into things enthusiastically, including writing assignments, and learn best in active learning situations that are filled with movement and variety. Because of this, they may get frustrated with long tasks that require a lot of reading and reflection.

Intuition-Sensation

Do you consider yourself to be more of a practical person or an innovative person? Is it easier for you to learn facts or concepts? This dimension tells you about how you perceive information in your environment.

Intuition (N). Intuition refers to use of the "sixth sense," or unconscious way of knowing the world. Intuitive people learn best when instruction is open-ended with a focus on theory before application. Intuitive learning can be characterized as a creative, right-brain approach to learning. Intuitive learners often work in bursts of energy that yield quick flashes of insight. The intuitive learner wants and needs to see how everything works together; they look at the big picture. They tend to engage in divergent thinking as opposed to convergent thinking. Creative approaches to writing are preferred, and writing tends to be full of generalities (and facts might not be too accurate!). On multiple-choice tests, intuitive learners follow their hunches but can make errors involving facts (too many details can bore them). If you happen to be an intuitive learner, it is a good idea to read each question twice to make sure you read it correctly. Intuitive learners may be negligent about details at times, but they are generally good at drawing inferences when reading. They prefer to read something that gives them ideas to daydream about.

Sensation (S). Sensing refers to the process of acquiring information through your five senses (sight, sound, smell, touch, and taste). Sensing people learn best when there is an orderly sequencing of material that moves slowly from concrete to abstract. Sensing people prefer to process concrete, factual information and can become impatient with theories or examples that are not oriented to the present. In an academic setting, they tend to work steadily and focus on details and facts. If not aware of this tendency when reading and taking notes, they can end up neglecting important concepts and miss the broader picture. When completing a writing assignment, sensing persons prefer explicit, detailed directions. They prefer to read something that teaches new facts or tells how to do something. Sensing people are good at memorizing facts, and on multiple-choice tests they search for clues that relate to practical knowledge and personal experience. Because they rarely trust their hunches, they generally lose points by changing answers.

Thinking-Feeling

When you make a decision, do you tend to be more impersonal and objective or personal and subjective? We all use our cognitions (thoughts) and emotions (feelings) when making decisions, but we generally use one more than the other.

Thinking (T). Thinking people tend to discover and gather facts first and then make decisions based on logic. They enjoy problem solving, analyzing situations, weighing the pros and cons, and developing models for deeper understanding. In writing assignments they are task-oriented, organizing thoughts and focusing on content. When reading, they tend to engage in critical thinking and can stay engaged in reading even if the information does not personally engage them.

Feeling (F). Feeling people tend to make decisions based on feelings, values, and empathy. Feeling types are motivated by personal encouragement, and in making decisions, they consider the effect of the impact of the decision on others. In writing they tend to rely on personal experience and focus on the message and how it will affect the reader. In reading, they prefer material that is personally engaging; otherwise, there is a chance they will become bored and quit reading.

Perceiving-Judging

Once decisions have been made, based on thoughts and feelings, how do you act on them? Do you seek closure and act quickly, or do you prefer to keep your options open and maybe even procrastinate?

Perceiving (P). Perceivers tend to be adaptable and spontaneous, preferring open, spontaneous learning situations. They like gathering additional information before acting on a decision and because of their flexible, tentative nature, they are good at seeing multiple perspectives. Perceiving types tend to start many tasks at once and tend not to be good with deadlines. They prefer the process more than the completion of the task, can easily get distracted, and often need help in organizing. On multiple-choice tests, each answer can be a stimulus for more thought (gathering more information), so it is often difficult for the perceiver to choose the correct answer. When writing, perceivers tend to choose expansive topics that sometimes do not have a clear focus.

Judging (J). The judging type wants to get things settled and wrapped up. Judging types are goal-oriented and generally set manageable goals. Their first drafts tend to be short and underdeveloped. When reading, judging types may be too quick to interpret a book. They tend to gauge their learning by how many pages they have read or how much time they have spent on it. They generally enjoy planning and organizing and prefer to work on one task at a time. Judging types prefer well-defined goals and get frustrated with a lot of ambiguity.

Personality clearly affects learning patterns. In Exercise 1, the score for each personality dimension suggests the extent to which that dimension affects your learning style. In the process of discovering your learning style, try to see if it matches your professor's teaching style. If your professor goes about lecturing in a round-about way, using metaphors and analogies, trying to get you to see the big picture through theories and concepts, an intuitive teaching style is being used. If you are a sensing student who wants facts presented in an orderly, sequential manner beginning with concrete information, you may have to adapt your learning style to avoid feeling frustrated and discouraged. If your teacher presents a lot of facts and detailed information in a sequential, organized lecture format, a sensing teaching style is being used. If you are an intuitive learner who needs examples and theories first, you will need to adapt your learning style so as not to become bored and start daydreaming in class. Students who are sensing and judging (SJ) have a strong need for order and thus need a lot of structure in learning. Students who are intuitive and perceiving (NP) need more creative and autonomous learning situations. In a perfect world, teachers' teaching styles and students' learning styles would match, but as we all know, this is not a perfect world. The Swiss developmental psychologist Piaget wrote much about the power of adaptation. *Adaptation* is making adjustments to fit a new situation. We do it all the time as we assimilate new information into preexisting learning patterns. The more flexible your learning style, the greater your capacity to learn.

YOUR OWN PERSONAL LEARNING STYLE

Learning styles are very individual. Your task is to take responsibility for your own learning and discover different ways of studying that work for you so you can take advantage of your brain's incredible capacity for learning. Your own personal learning style is based on brain dominance, perceptual learning modalities, personality, and also environmental factors.

Your learning environment also affects your ability to think and learn. What environment is most conducive to learning for you? Do you need a quiet place like an upper floor of the library where little noise is tolerated? Do you prefer a place where you know there will be people and lots of action? Did you know that some people find that they can concentrate best when music is playing softly in the background? The steady rhythms of baroque music from the sixteenth through eighteenth century (e.g., Mozart, Handel, Corelli, Pachelbel, and Vivaldi) seem to work best. This music tends to keep the body relaxed while the mind remains alert, ready to process new information (except for music majors who may be tempted to analyze the music!). What time of the day are you most alert? What energizes you and what zaps you of your energy when studying?

Reflecting on your answers to these questions as well as becoming aware of all variables that affect your own unique learning patterns can enable you to become a more efficient, effective learner. Think and study in ways that match your learning style. Maximize your learning potential.

SOURCES

Buzan, T. (1976). *Use both sides of your brain.* New York: E. P. Dutton.

Gardner, H. (1993). *Multiple intelligences: The theory in practice.* New York: Basic Books.

James, W. B., & Galbraith, M. W. (1985). Perceptual learning styles: Implications and techniques for the practitioner. *Lifelong Learning, 8,* 20–23.

Keirsey, D., & Bates, M. (1984). *Please understand me.* Del Mar, CA: Prometheus.

Myers, I. (1995). *Gifts differing.* Palo Alto, CA: Davies-Black.

Sacks, O. (1970). *The man who mistook his wife for a hat and other clinical tales.* New York: Harper Perennial.

Sperry, R. W. (1974). Lateral specialization in the surgically separated hemispheres. In F. O. Schmitt & R. G. Worden (Eds.), *The neurosciences third study programs* (pp. 5–19). Cambridge, MA: MIT Press.

Wonder, J., & Donovan, P. (1984). *Whole-brain thinking.* New York: William Morrow.

NAME: _____ DATE: _____

EXERCISE 1. DISCOVERING YOUR PERSONALITY TYPE

Put a check next to any statements that describe you.

EXTROVERT

_____ Enjoys interacting with others while learning

_____ Tends to jump into things enthusiastically

_____ Uses a trial-and-error approach to problem solving

_____ Enjoys group discussions and group projects

_____ Prefers active learning situations full of movement and variety

INTROVERT

_____ Prefers to work alone

_____ Likes to spend time thinking and reflecting before acting

_____ Thinks best in relative solitude

_____ Content working alone on lengthy projects

_____ Prefers to work with ideas

INTUITION

_____ Works in bursts of energy followed by not so productive periods

_____ Enjoys learning a new approach more than using it

_____ Tends to be good at solving novel problems

_____ Often impatient with routine procedures

_____ Prefers to focus on concepts and may neglect the details

_____ Wants to see the big picture

SENSATION

_____ Works steadily

_____ Learns best when starting with the concrete and moving to the abstract

_____ Prefers explicit, detailed directions

_____ Patient with routine procedures

_____ Tends to focus on facts and may miss overall concepts

_____ Values accuracy and precision

THINKING

_____ Tends to be logical and analytical

_____ Prefers to discover and gather facts before making decisions

_____ Weighs pros and cons of a situation

_____ Interested in what is just

FEELING

_____ Tends to make decision based on feelings and values

_____ Considers other's feelings before making decisions

_____ Motivated by personal encouragement

_____ Interested in reconciliation

PERCEIVING	JUDGING
_____ Adapts easily to changes	_____ May not adapt easily to change
_____ May tend to procrastinate	_____ Prefers to make decisions quickly
_____ Prefers open, spontaneous learning situations	_____ Prefers to follow a plan
_____ Tends to see all sides of an issue	_____ Remains on task

Evaluation

Answer the following questions by circling the appropriate letter.

Did you have more checks next to statements about extroverts (E) or introverts (I)?   E   I

Did you have more checks next to statements about sensation (S) or intuition (N)?   S   N

Did you have more checks next to statements about thinking (T) or feeling (F)?   T   F

Did you have more checks next to statements about perceiving (P) or judging (J)?   P   J

What is your personality type (write four letters)? _____ _____ _____ _____

EXERCISE 2. PERSONAL LEARNING STYLE

1. Do you think you are more right-brain or left-brain? Why?

2. When solving a problem, how can you engage in a whole-brain approach?

3. What are your primary and secondary perceptual learning modalities?

4. What learning strategies can you use to capitalize on these modalities?

5. What is your personality type? ____ ____ ____ ____ (Refer to Exercise 1.)

   How does your personality type relate to your perceptual learning modalities and your brain dominance?

EXERCISE 2 (continued)

6.   Describe your perfect study environment.

7.   What changes do you need to make right now to become a more efficient and effective learner?

Chapter 4

Stress

Accentuate the Positive

Everyone knows when he or she is experiencing stress, and each one of us can discuss various stressors that confront us each week. A **stressor**, according to Hans Selye, is anything that produces tension in your life, which may be of a physical nature (e.g., starvation brought on by a drought in east Africa, restricted access to a friend's house caused by a broken leg in a cast) or a psychological nature (e.g., being involved in interpersonal conflict, being frustrated in a second attempt to pass a required course). Of these two categories, it seems that psychological stressors are forever present, even in the best of times, for most students. Psychological stressors confront us all regardless of how healthy, powerful, or rich we are, although these stressors differ in the degree to which they "stress us out."

Stress often arises when we have choices to make. In most cases we would rather deal with selecting between two goods than two evils, but conflict can be experienced when one is selecting between two attractive outcomes. Such an **approach-approach** type of conflict might involve having to select between two high-paying jobs after graduating from college. While approach-approach conflicts are unlikely to end like the one in the example known as "Buridan's ass," where a donkey caught between two equally attractive piles of hay dies from being unable to decide which pile to eat, conflict is conflict, and even selecting between two desirables can be stressful.

Memories concerning our struggle to choose between two evils seem to be vivid and lasting. For example, a person choosing between taking out a student loan with a high interest rate or asking his or her parents for additional help knowing they can ill afford the assistance is in this situation. Having two dreadful choices is commonly referred to as being caught "between a rock and a hard spot." The person is experiencing an **avoidance-avoidance** type of conflict. No matter what the cause, psychological frustration can be profoundly stressful and may even cause us to respond aggressively. We might scream at our roommate or even become physically violent in extreme cases of stress.

If asked, all of us could easily list stressful events or periods in our life (e.g., death of a pet, moving from one school or town to another, loss of a close family member through death, divorce of parents, loss of some prized possession, enrolling in college classes for the first time). Stress can be defined as a personal experience of physical or mental strain that results in numerous physiological changes (e.g., heart-rate increases, increase in the force of one's heartbeat, digestive disturbance, blood-vessel constriction, elevated blood pressure, noticeable sweating, rise in muscle tightness). In this chapter we will discuss the causes and symptoms of stress and how you can develop effective ways to cope with stress.

WHAT IS STRESS EXACTLY?

The items listed on the assessment tool developed by Holmes and Rahe help us understand what the term stress encompasses in everyday language. Simply stated, stress is a reaction to the various things that happen to us, both negative and positive. Interestingly, while most of us readily think of negative events as stress-provoking (e.g., jail term, death of a close friend, being fired at work), in reality events that are very positive in nature can also be stressful (e.g., change in residence, vacation, marriage). Even though we might be able to cite exceptions, in the vast majority of cases one's wedding day is a joyful event marked by celebration. Marriage also introduces many changes for both people involved. Issues can range from who pays for which day-to-day living expense to the "correct" way to squeeze toothpaste from a tube. Changes associated with marriage can generate a lot of stress.

A meaningful and useful way to conceptualize stress is given in the following formula.

Stress = Number of Resources – Number of Changes

Thus, high levels of stress are due to changes exceeding resources, and low levels of stress are due to resources exceeding changes.

Holmes and Rahe's list of stressful events covers a wide range of the adult life span, although several of the items would not apply to many undergraduates. In a college environment one would expect to find certain changes not listed by Holmes and Rahe to be just as stressful as those listed. These could include dropping or being withdrawn from a class with a "W," receiving a $20 ticket from campus police for a parking violation, changing from one major to another, not being able to enter a major because of one's grade point average, being withdrawn from a course with a "WF," joining a sorority or fraternity, transferring to another college (leaving this college or coming to this college as a transfer student), failing a course in one's major with a "favorite" professor, first dismissal from college, and being accused of academic dishonesty. In the above equation, note that the word "change" is important. Frequently we are forced to deal with changes that wear us down physically and psychologically because we lack the necessary resources at the time to cope. Our store of coping resources can fluctuate. Remember the last time when you had the flu and experienced a drop in your ability to cope with the demands placed on you?

Not all change is bad; in fact, there is evidence to suggest that we need a certain amount of change to maintain our physical and psychological balance. Psychologists and other researchers once studied the effect of relatively unchanging surroundings (referred to as sensory deprivation studies). Participants were required to wear blindfolds or the equivalent, to stay still by lying down in soundproof rooms or large containers, to have their arms restrained in special devices to avoid experiencing tactile sensations, and so forth. The effects were profound in some cases; some participants even reported hallucinations.

While too much change is bad, too little can also be bad. Apparently, too few external changes result in the body creating self-induced changes (hallucinations). But we are all individuals, and it is important to recognize that individuals differ in how much change they can tolerate.

PSYCHOLOGICAL HARDINESS AND PERSONALITY DIFFERENCES

In *Man in Search of Meaning*, Victor Frankl describes how an individual can confront a truly unusual degree of change (incarceration in a concentration camp) and not only survive but come out stronger as a result. Perspective is very important in explaining outcomes, and we all differ in the degree to which we like change, or seek change in our lives. Some people seem to be revitalized by changes, and some even seek out high-pressure positions because of the constantly changing demands. Many presidents of the United States likely fall into this category of stress-hardy individuals. People such as Jimmy Carter, Elizabeth Dole, John Glenn, Hillary Clinton, Dianne Feinstein, George W. Bush, and Christine Whitman who are serving or have served in high-profile positions in politics probably all possess a high level of psychological hardiness. For example, when Senator Feinstein was asked whether she would consider running for president, she said:

> *I've been the first [woman] four times now: once as president of the Board of Supervisors [in San Francisco], as mayor, as the first gubernatorial candidate in my state, the first woman Senator from my state. What I've learned is there is a testing period that goes on—particularly in an executive capacity. I think it [takes someone] with the ability to run a campaign well, put together a platform that resounds with the American people and someone with the stamina, the staying power, the determination and enthusiasm to carry it off. (Ciabattari, 1999, p. 6)*

Psychological hardiness is reflected in individuals who like and seek change and challenges, possess a clear focus or goal, and perceive themselves as having control.

Stressful events can be short in duration (e.g., writing a speech) or long (e.g., a difficult job with a lot of responsibilities), but it is not always the magnitude of the event that determines how well we cope. The same stressors might be tolerable for one person but overwhelming to another. Our personal level of psychological hardiness is very important. Salvatore Maddi and Suzanne Kobasa (1994) studied executives in stressful situations, primarily due to an organization undergoing reorganization with the possibility of lost employment. Such periods of reorganization are associated with ill health (increases colds, influenza, backaches, and migraine headaches). Maddi and Kobasa found that some individuals were not as susceptible to the reorganization stressor. These resilient individuals were able to maintain a sense of control over most events encountered in life. The psychologically hardy displayed few of the effects found in others. The researchers found that the psychologically hardy (PH) possess

- An open attitude toward change, assessing *change as a challenge* rather than a threat to one's self.

- *A high degree of commitment* to what the person is involved in. This commitment is tied to goals and objectives. Subjects low in commitment tended to display evidence of being alienated from work, people, and things.
- *A sense of control over most events* rather than a sense of helplessness. High PHs are convinced they can influence the course of their future. In their eyes, effort makes a difference at work, in school, and in relationships. Low PHs felt they had little if any power to influence outcomes. For this latter group, outside forces controlled their future.

One of the lessons to be learned from the work of Maddi and Kobasa is that individuals confronted with stress can meet it head on (take active steps) or let the situation roll over them (take a passive approach). In the latter case, the person does not see the situation as a challenge, but rather as a threat beyond his or her control. In some cases, rather than being able to call upon a sense of commitment to sustain them during a difficult period, individuals low on hardiness worry and try to escape; they may deny what is occurring or even blame others. The following list summarizes the differences between high PH and low PH.

High PH	Low PH
Sees a challenge	Sees a threat
Commitment	Alienation
Active coping	Passive coping
Seeks change	Avoids change
Feels invigorated	Feels helpless

Martin Seligman (1995) has coined the term **learned helplessness**. Specifically, Seligman used the term to refer to situations where a person (or animal, since a lot of studies in this area use animal subjects) acts in a helpless manner if exposed to situations that are harmful or painful *and cannot be avoided.* The unavoidability of these situations seems to inhibit learning how to escape a harmful or painful situation in the future—a situation that could be avoided. In one early study on learned helplessness, dogs were placed in one of two treatments. Those in treatment A were confined to a harness and given electric shocks without any possibility of escape. Those in treatment B were exposed to the same exact conditions except if the animal struggled it could escape. Treatment A led to the dogs becoming less competitive, less aggressive, and less able to escape painful situations in the future. Treatment B resulted in dogs who were more competitive, aggressive, and better capable of escaping painful situations in the future. Other animal experiments on mice and rats produced animals in the learned helplessness group who were less active, displayed greater difficulty learning, and gave up sooner when confronted with challenges. Human participants in similar studies were found to be affected adversely in terms of problem-solving ability.

In general, from the numerous studies conducted it appears that some humans, due to certain experiences in and outside the academic world, "learn to be helpless." The effects of learned helplessness follow.

- The ability to effectively solve problems is reduced. A drop in motivation, energy, and the will to struggle and survive occurs.
- Learning becomes much more difficult. People ignore or seem unable to profit from information.
- An elevation of emotional or physical distress occurs. Individuals are likely to show outward signs of anxiety and depression. If conditions are not altered, the person may become sick or develop an illness (similar to Holmes and Rahe's findings that also uncovered a relationship between stressful conditions and illness).

Finally, an individual's personality type influences how much stress the person may experience. For example, while anxiety can be a symptom of stress and anxiety levels vary from day to day and week to week (called state anxiety), individuals also display somewhat consistent patterns (called trait anxiety). Charles Spielberger (1972) identified these two categories and uncovered some interesting findings. While the announcement of an important test can be expected to alter one's level of state anxiety, individuals differ in how much it affects them. These differences are related to the personality of the individual. Individuals with low trait anxiety usually seem calm and laid-back, while individuals with high trait anxiety typically seem high-strung and are frequently worried. Keep in mind that anxiety is not in and of itself bad—it serves to motivate us to study. Both high-anxiety and low-anxiety individuals may experience performance problems but for different reasons; in the former case, the high level of anxiety hinders processing of information, and in the latter, there is too little anxiety to motivate the person to study adequately.

Another type of personality that has been linked to stress is the **Type A personality**. Type A personalities are stress generators, creating stress in addition to what is placed on them from the outside. Type A personalities are driven to work (often working long hours, weekends), very goal conscious (frequently thinking of goals that need to be achieved and tasks that need to be completed), and find it very difficult to relax. This type of person always seems to be in a rush and may tend to finish others' sentences. Type A personalities find it very difficult to settle for less than perfection. Behind the wheel of a car, Type A personalities are likely to become agitated or angry because other drivers are "moving too slow," preventing the Type A from getting to his or her destination. The advantage of being a Type A is achievement (higher grades); the disadvantage is poor health (they tend to be more susceptible to heart attacks).

PROLONGED STRESS AND IMPAIRMENT OF FUNCTIONING

Clearly, stress can be generated in many different ways, and we know from Holmes and Rahe's work that high levels of stress can result in illness and dysfunction. Does this happen overnight? The good news is no. The effects tend to accumulate over time, which means we have a period of time to take action to prevent the worst-case scenario from occurring. According to Hans Selye, when responding to stress, we go through a series of stages called the General Adaptation Syndrome (GAS).

Stage 1: Alarm (Fight/Flight)

Stress leads to physiological changes in your body (e.g., heart rate and respiration increase, adrenaline levels rise, and digestive functions drop). The body is gearing itself up to take action. The person prepares to either "*fight or take flight,*" that is, run from a perceived danger.

Stage 2: Resistance

Our "fight or flight" response has its origins in our early history as humans two million or more years ago. The problem is we are no longer literally fighting or running from saber-toothed tigers. We can neither punch the rude, unreasonable professor nor run out of his required class. Often we must stay put and endure the stressors in our life and suffer the consequences (in the twenty-first century the "fight or flight" response we are physiologically and mentally prepared to carry out is no longer appropriate in many situations). When we are stuck between fight and flight, the physiological changes that occur in the alarm stage still occur but at a lower level. But this level is still strong enough to wear us down psychologically and physically.

Stage 3: Exhaustion

At this point our resources are low and physical deterioration can set in (possibly contributing to conditions such as heart disease, hypertension, asthma, colitis, and, according to some researchers, ulcers and some forms of cancer). These diseases of adaptation or psychosomatic illnesses are the result of the person being blocked from reacting to a problem in a manner that can reestablish his or her equilibrium.

Too much adrenaline is associated with a drop in white blood cells, which impacts the immune system. For many students, prolonged stress results in symptoms such as fatigue, boredom, less restful sleep, loss of appetite (or eating much more), agitation, and becoming prone to making mistakes and having accidents. It has been estimated that over 45% of headaches are stress related.

WHAT CAN BE DONE?

Many students (and nonstudents) respond to stress in self-defeating ways, by using drugs and alcohol, withdrawing from the things that are important but cause stress, and using psychological defenses such as denial, projection, or fantasizing. In fact, there are many things that can be done to relieve and prevent stress. Here are several suggestions that we have found effective and relatively easy to apply.

Everyday Techniques for Reducing Stress

Check your gauges (psychological/emotional, behavioral, and physical). Periodically stop and determine how much stress you are experiencing. Is it high or low? Whatever the level is, is the stress having a negative impact on your academic performance, your personal life, or your ability to just enjoy life? Sometimes such self-examination leads to the awareness that there are some unnecessary sources of stress in your life. For example, perhaps an acquaintance is always putting you down in subtle ways but denies doing so; no one should go through life maintaining such an association. If confronting the person does not change the situation, it is probably better to break off the relationship.

Feed yourself psychologically and emotionally. Read that book you have wanted to get to, listen to your favorite music, go to a movie or the local mall, start a hobby, or get involved in a community service such as Habitat for Humanity. It is important to take time to get away. While a stressed-out student may find it difficult to find the time to get away, such time-outs can replenish one's depleted energy and help break the cycle of lingering stress (i.e., GAS).

Feed yourself physiologically and behaviorally. Exercise. Spend 30 minutes three times a week. Take advantage of the college exercise facility if one is available; play tennis, racquetball, handball, basketball, and learn mountain climbing. Joining a team also helps to establish a support system. If you are on a tight schedule and cannot take time to travel somewhere, walk or run a mile or more a day near your residence (walk or run with a trusted partner so you are not out alone), or ride a bike on campus and climb the stairs in a campus building rather than riding the elevator. Not only is health improved by exercise, but exercise has been proven to reduce stress levels. Of course, adequate sleep and good nutrition are necessary ingredients in managing anxiety and stress.

Breathe deeply. During periods of stress take a moment to close your eyes. Breathe in two or three times in a slow and deep manner, allowing your stomach to rise as you breathe in. Slowly exhale through your lips. Increasing one's oxygen level in this manner can help relieve stress.

Divert your attention. Waiting for the professor to distribute a test to the class or to be called on to make a presentation can elevate your anxiety and stress level. Instead of sitting there thinking negative thoughts ("I am not sure I am prepared"), bump the negative thoughts aside with a pleasant image (visualize your favorite vacation spot) or focus on an available image (the tree outside the window that is swaying in the breeze). A simple refocusing from negative thoughts to something more pleasant in nature has been found to reduce anxiety and stress.

Visualize success. When feeling anxious due to some stressor (e.g., a major course paper that is due), visualize yourself as being successful. Visualize the various steps necessary in a task and actually picture yourself being successful each step of the way. A student teacher might go to the classroom where he or she will be teaching and go through the lesson plan without students there. He or she might use the chalkboard, read from the text, and so forth, all the while imagining a positive outcome. Such an activity has proven to be effective in reducing one's level of anxiety and stress.

Apply environmental engineering tactics. Make your apartment, dorm room, or house a relaxing environment. Decorate the walls with favorite posters or pictures, place objects around that elicit pleasant memories or feelings, purchase a tropical fish tank, which can help to create a soothing environment. Have a place that can be your place to escape to and fill it with items that make you feel good.

Techniques for Periods of High Stress

During periods of high stress we typically find it much more effective to develop an ongoing routine that involves cognitive restructuring, muscle relaxation, meditation, or sequential imagery. Such techniques are intended to be learned and practiced on a regular basis.

Cognitive Restructuring. Sometimes students are aware they are their own worst enemy because of negative self-talk. These are messages that a person repeats to himself or herself that negatively affect both performance and quality of life. Both test-anxious and non-test-anxious students say negative things to themselves (e.g., "I am going to fail this test!"), but test-anxious students make such remarks much more frequently and tend to believe them more. Albert Ellis, the creator of rational emotive behavior therapy, has had considerable success in having people tackle their stress-producing thoughts using an A-B-C approach to modifying behavior.

> A = **activating event,** which can be thought of as the stressor ("I have an important test Tuesday"). The event in and of itself is not the problem; it is how we perceive the event that is crucial.
>
> B = **belief** about the activating event. If my belief is that I will fail the test, then I will experience unnecessary stress.
>
> C = **consequence.** If I perceive myself as failing, I will experience stress and thus become anxious and not perform at my optimum level. We can alter the process at point B by forcefully injecting more positive thoughts to push out the self-defeating ones we have come accustomed to speaking silently to ourselves.

Ellis emphasizes that our irrational thinking generates a great deal of stress that simply does not reflect reality. This view is captured in the story of the man who discloses the following when reflecting back about his long life: "I am an old man who has had many worries in my life, few of which ever came true."

Imagery. Imaging exercises can also break the cycle of negative self-talk but do so with images, not words. For example, a person may practice sequentially going through a certain set of positive images for 10 minutes or longer. During a period of stress (e.g., waiting for a test to be distributed in class), the person can call upon one of the images used to reduce anxiety on the spot.

An example of imaging exercise follows. Read over the following images and then close your eyes and imagine the scene described.

> It is a beautiful spring day.
> Out my window I can see a crystal-clear, deep-blue sky.
> Almost as in a dream I go to my front door and step outside.
> There is a gentle breeze.
> The smell of flowers and the sound of singing birds are very pleasant.
> I walk out onto the fresh, green grass.
> I slowly kneel down and decide to lie back on the fresh, spring grass.
> The temperature is just right.

I start to daydream about a trip to my favorite beach.

I see myself on the beach and the sun is not too bright, just nice and warm.

The water is a beautiful aqua color that I can see through to the bottom.

The sand on the beach is a beautiful white, and coconut trees are spread out up and down the beach.

I start to walk on the beach.

The sound of the waves is very soothing.

The saltwater smell is refreshing.

I stop when I notice a seashell embedded in the sand. It has many bright colors.

Reds.

Yellows.

Blues.

I bend over and pick up the beautifully colored shell.

The feel of the water-worn shell is comforting.

The sun is going down and is near the horizon.

I sit down on the sand to watch the sun set.

It is a beautiful sunset with various shades of reds, and I feel warm and at peace.

A deep sense of peace flows over me, and I have no fears or worries.

I return from my imaginary trip feeling both very relaxed and revitalized, as if I just enjoyed a long, restful sleep from which I open my eyes and feel great and optimistic about the world.

Deep Relaxation. For this exercise it is recommended that you practice approximately 20 minutes per day for about two weeks to master the technique. In a quiet, disturbance-free location, you are to go through the following muscle groups, tensing and relaxing them. The technique teaches a person, without going through the whole procedure, to quickly scan the body in approximately 10 seconds to locate pockets of muscle tension, which are then relaxed. The resulting state of relaxation can bring about a significant reduction in anxiety and stress allowing the person to focus his or her attention without having negative thoughts intrude. Keep in mind that when practicing this technique, you should not strain any part of the body that has been injured or is recovering from injury.

Lie back in a bed (or on the floor). Place a pillow under your head. After taking three deep breaths as described earlier, do the following:

Close your eyes.

Clench both your fists. Study the tension.

Relax the fingers of your hands and study the difference.

Enjoy the feeling of just lying there relaxed.

Again, clench both hands tighter and tighter. Study and focus on the tension you created in this part of your body.

Allow yourself to become relaxed all over.

Bend your elbows. Feel the tension created by bending your elbows. Dwell on the tension. Get to know how the tension feels in this part of the body.

Allow yourself to become very relaxed all over.

Become more and more relaxed. Imagine that you are so relaxed that you are sinking into the surface beneath you.

Straighten your arms out. Feel the tension created by pushing your arms straight out.

Now relax your arms and let them find their own place.

Wrinkle your forehead. Examine how the wrinkles feel and picture how they look. Now relax. Let the wrinkles go and picture in your mind the way your forehead now looks without the wrinkles.

Squeeze your eyes shut. Experience the tension you created using your eyes. Relax your eyes.

Relax all over.

Stay as relaxed as possible for about a minute.

Relax.

Relax.

Now clamp your teeth together. Study the tension created by biting your teeth together. Tension is being created in the jaws. Picture in your mind how the muscles in this area are tight.

Relax.

Now press your head back—push back on the pillow. Now stop and allow your body to become comfortable all over. Picture your body melting into the surface of the bed (or floor). Your body is so relaxed it is sinking down.

It is like you are a big rag doll just lying there.

Relax.

Move your head down so it is now against your chest. Study the tension that this movement created.

Relax.

Bring you shoulders up. Study the muscle tension created when you try to touch your ears with your shoulders.

Relax.

Now pull in your stomach, tighter and tighter. Now relax.

Relax.

Create a small arch in your back. Feel the tension in your muscles when you arch your back. Relax and allow your back to settle into a comfortable position as you do when you go to sleep at night.

Point your toes up toward the top of your head. Maintain this for 20 seconds. Now relax.

Relax.

Point your toes away from the top of your head. Maintain this position for about 10 seconds. Now relax.

Relax.

Raise one leg. Keep the leg up until the tension starts to become uncomfortable. Now lower that leg.

Relax.

Now lift the other leg. Keep it up for about the same length of time. Okay, now relax.

Become as relaxed as you are capable of becoming. Release all the muscle tension in your body. Relax more and more until you reach a very relaxed state—a very, very deep state of relaxation.

Lie there in a relaxed state for a while.

Now *imagine* getting up (*do not move*—just imagine getting up.) Notice the change in muscle tension even when you just picture in your mind that you are getting up.

Go back to a deep state of relaxation. Let any tension you find pour out of your body as if you were a bucket with many, many holes and the tension is water.

After about a minute permit yourself to come out of your relaxed state. You will feel refreshed upon getting up from where you were lying.

Meditation. There are various meditation techniques that can be used. A basic ingredient is to clear one's mind of thoughts and to concentrate on breathing. For example, as a person breathes in, he or she should count *one* for the *breath in, two* for the *breath out, three* for the next *breath in.* Continue all the way to the number *ten.* The trick is not to allow stray thoughts or images to occupy your mind. If this occurs, you must start over with the number one. It sounds easy—it is not. Try this exercise. It will take a period of practice (sometimes a long period) before you can reach the number ten without some sort of intrusion into your mind. Emptying one's mind is difficult.

In part, meditation is a way to slow us down. The mind is sometimes described as "a bunch of monkeys jumping from tree to tree," a metaphor to reflect how cluttered our mind can be with all the thoughts that enter its domain, disturbing its peace. As early as the 1970s, Herbert Benson and his colleagues at Harvard Medical School (see *The Relaxation Response,* 1975) found that by passively clearing the mind during meditation, oxygen requirements drop, heartbeat slows, blood pressure lowers, and we experience a mental and physiological calmness.

SOURCES

Barrios, B. A., Ginter, E. J., Scalise, J. J., & Miller, F. G. (1980). Treatment of test anxiety by applied relaxation and cue-controlled relaxation. *Psychological Reports, 46,* 1287–1296.

Benson, H. (1975). *The relaxation response.* New York: Morrow.

Ciabattari, J. (1999, January). Women who could be president. *Parade Magazine,* 6–7.

Ellis, A., & Grieger, R. (Eds.) (1977). *Handbook of rational emotive therapy.* New York: Springer.

Friedman, M., & Rosenman, R. H. (1974). *Type A behavior and your heart.* New York: Knopf.

Glauser, A., & Glauser, E. (2001). *Cultivating the spirit of mindfulness in counseling and psychotherapy.* Presentation made at the 2001 World Conference of the American Counseling Association, San Antonio, TX.

Maddi, S. R., & Hess, M. J. (1992). Personality hardiness and success in basketball. *International Journal of Sport Psychology, 23,* 360–368.

Maddi, S. R., & Kosaba, D. M. (1994). Hardiness and mental health. *Journal of Personality Assessment, 64,* 265–274.

Seligman, M. E. P. (1975). *Helplessness: On depression, development, and death.* San Francisco: W. H. Freeman.

Selye, H. (1953). *The Stress of Life.* New York: Knopf.

Spielberger, C. D. (Ed.). (1972). *Anxiety: Current trends in theory and research.* New York: Academic Press.

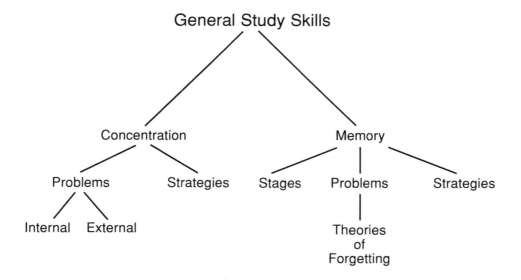

General Study Skills

Concentration

Problems

Internal   External

Strategies

Memory

Stages   Problems   Strategies

Theories
of
Forgetting

Chapter 5

Remembering to Concentrate

Concentration and memory are both important factors in your learning process. The ability to concentrate affects how much you can accomplish while you are studying. The ability to remember information is going to determine how well you will be able to apply this information in your life and how well you will score on tests.

Concentration is a by-product. It only happens when we don't think about it. If you are engrossed in a Civil War battle in your history book and suddenly realize that you were concentrating, then at that moment you would have broken your concentration on the battle.

Concentration is the process that permits you to focus your attention on a particular task. This process requires continual monitoring of distractors. You will have a better chance of improving your concentration if you know what causes you to lose it.

WHY IS CONCENTRATION DIFFICULT?

Concentrating on a subject is not something that just "happens." Albert Einstein was the typical "absent-minded professor." His enormous intellectual powers were so concentrated on the problem at hand that he lost all connection with routine activities. A good example today would be the teenager engrossed in playing a video game. He loses all touch with routine activities. "I can't concentrate" is a common student complaint. The habit of concentration can be developed by self-discipline and practice in "becoming involved."

WHAT ARE SOME PROBLEMS IN CONCENTRATING AND THEIR SOLUTIONS?

1.   *Problem:* Mental and/or Physical Fatigue—It is difficult to concentrate when you are tired. Studying late at night can be a problem because of this. Mental fatigue can be caused by too many things to do, depression, fear of failure, lack of interest, and many more factors. When you are physically tired, it is hard to care about anything, not to mention trying to concentrate on it. Sometimes boredom can be the cause of the fatigue feeling.

     Solution: Determine the time of day you are most alert. Use this time of day for your most difficult assignments. A proper diet, rest, and exercise will also help you be more alert. If boredom is the culprit, find something in the class that will help you build an interest. Look until you find it! Be alert to ways in which your class relates to your life. Read actively and converse mentally with the author. It also helps to study in a well-ventilated room. Take short breaks and do something active.

2.   *Problem:* Too Much to Do—Procrastination is usually the cause here. Often we are more overwhelmed by the idea of all that we need to do than the actual work that needs to be accomplished. When we try to think of several things at once, it is impossible to concentrate.

     Solution: Keep a calendar of test and assignment deadlines. The deadline for one class will probably coincide with the deadline of another class. Make a schedule with definite times for studying and completing specific assignments. Stick to this schedule! One way to do this is to set goals for each study session. Plan ahead exactly what you expect to accomplish in that session. It is important to set realistic goals. Divide long assignments into short sessions. Reward yourself after your objective is completed. Your objective should not be to just cover the pages, but to understand the assignment.

3.   *Problem:* A Poor Attitude—If you do not care about what you are studying, you obviously will not be able to concentrate!

     Solution: Accept the fact you need to learn the material. Many people have spent long hours in deciding what courses were necessary to fit a particular program. Decisions are not always based on simply turning out good teachers or lawyers. These people were also concerned with producing good, well-rounded individuals.

     Before you allow your attitude to ruin any hope of good concentration and retention, give the subject a chance. Be an active reader. Dig in and question, agree, or disagree with the author. Talk to students who are majoring in this field and see what interests them. Could it be possible that your lack of background is causing the dislike? Explore this field in an encyclopedia. Look in bookstores for review and workbooks. If you can build a background, maybe you can help your attitude!

4. *Problem:* No Concentration Habit—If you have been out of school for a period of time, did not apply yourself previously, or have not been involved in an activity that required concentration, maybe you have "lost" the habit of concentration.

   Solution: You had it at one time. You have concentrated when you were learning to ride a bicycle, when you learned to read and write, drive a car, and many other basic skills you possess. You can re-develop this skill by being aware of how important it is. This could take some practice!

5. *Problem:* Noisy Study Environment—Are you trying to study with your favorite television program? How about your favorite music? Do you take your textbook to a ball game?

   Solution: Two or three hours of study in quiet surroundings does more good than ten hours of study in a noisy place. It is important to have a designated study place that is used only for studying. Concentrating will be aided by associating studying with a particular locale.

6. *Problem:* Poor Reading and Study Skills—It is difficult to concentrate if you are having problems understanding what you are trying to learn.

   Solution: If your vocabulary is limited, you need to work on this! Practice vocabulary exercises, word games, and read as much varied material as you can. You improve reading by reading. Learn basic effective approaches to textbook study.

7. *Problem:* Deciding Who Is in Control—It is difficult to concentrate if you're not aware of who controls your concentration efforts.

   Solution: You should be cognizant of what contributes to your concentration. If you are in control, then you are the one who can make the decisions necessary to increase your concentration. If the control is something else, is there anything you can do?

WHAT ARE EXTERNAL AND INTERNAL DISTRACTORS?

A learner must be able to cope with internal and external distractors before starting to concentrate and learn.

Internal Distractors

Any form of negative self-talk is an internal distractor. In order to concentrate, your mind must be quiet and controlled. Sometimes a small voice inside that should be full of confidence blurts out, "You are probably going to say something stupid," and, sure enough, this proves to be true. But luckily, there is also another voice hiding in there. You feel confident and knowledgeable about what you are about to say, and it comes out right! These inside voices determine to a great extent the "tone" of your world—whether it is good, bad, or indifferent. We can change how we feel by what we say to ourselves.

Negative self-talk can be produced by insecurity, fear, anxiety, frustration, defeatist attitudes, indecision, anger, daydreams, and personal problems. This self-talk is obviously influenced by your feelings. If your self-talk seems to lean more on the negative side, you are not alone! Richard Fenker says 80–90 percent of students with learning problems have self-talk that is predominantly negative. Fenker believes you can control these negative voices using your right brain and substituting more positive self-talk. If you are afraid of speaking in public, imagine yourself giving a report in front of a class. If you have test anxiety, imagine or picture yourself being relaxed and calm in that testing situation. Spend a few days listening to yourself. When a negative opinion surfaces, try to replace it with a neutral or a positive thought!

What Internal Distractors Affect You?

Take a look at the following list of internal distractors. Do any of these distractors seem to be a problem for you? If so, note the possible answer for this distractor.

Hunger	Eat before you study.
Fatigue	Plan study time when you are most alert and get at least 7 to 8 hours of sleep. Don't forget some exercise!
Illness	Postpone until you feel better.
Worrying about grades or work	Try to focus on the task and better grades will be the result. Focus on work while you are at work.
Stress	Attempt to focus on what you are trying to accomplish.
Physical discomfort	Study in a comfortable place.
Not understanding assignment	Always clarify assignments before you start.
Personal problems	Make a note of the problem and tell yourself you will cope after you study.
Lack of interest	Try studying with someone else, find something that you can relate to, or look at related material.
Negative attitude	Remember negative thoughts take away from getting a job done! Convince yourself there is something positive in the class.

Please note that some of these distractors can be eliminated if you anticipate your needs!

External Distractors

External distractors originate outside of you. They are those things that draw your attention away from a learning task.

Take a look at the following list of external distractors. Do some of them seem familiar? Many of these problems can also be eliminated if you anticipate your needs.

Lack of proper materials	Before you start your study session, have paper, pencil, etc. in place.

A PROGRAM TO INCREASE CONCENTRATION WHILE STUDYING

Purpose

This program is designed to help you learn deep and effective concentration while studying.

How Does It Work?

Primarily by capitalizing on the concentration powers you already possess. This is done by developing an extremely strong association between one particular physical location (such as the desk in your room) and deep concentration on your studies.

What Must You Do?

To set up a strong association such as this, you must: Remove old associations that your "study spot" might have for you. This means removing pictures, telephones, souvenirs, etc. from your study area. When seated in your "study chair" only materials being studied at that moment should be seen. This sounds simple and in fact it is not extremely difficult, but it does require some self-discipline—especially at the beginning. You learn this new association by merely making sure that the only time you are in your study spot is when you are concentrating on your studies. Get up and move to another chair, or at least turn around in your chair so that you are looking at an entirely different set of visual stimuli every time your mind wanders, a friend comes in to talk, your roommate asks you a question, etc. Don't be discouraged if you have to change locations or turn around every few minutes for the first several days. It takes this long to develop this new association for most people. It's vital that you do absolutely nothing except concentrate while in your study spot. If you feel like letting your mind wander, go ahead . . . but make sure you move out of your study spot or turn around in your chair. Also, don't force concentration, or you'll end up associating your study spot with discomfort rather than concentration. Concentration is also helped if you switch study subjects every half hour or forty-five minutes, rather than working so long on one particular subject that you tire of studying for that course.

What Can You Expect?

Between 75 and 90 percent of the students who try this program find they can dramatically increase their periods of deep concentration within a period of a week or so, if they have been faithful to the system. Going from periods of concentration as short as two minutes to more than 45 minutes within several weeks is not at all unusual. But remember, the first three or four days will be the hardest, because it is during that time you will not notice much change. After the third or fourth day (assuming you have studied several hours each day), you will begin to notice a difference. Some students find the number of times they have to turn around in their chairs the first few days to be discouraging, and feel that the system results in their wasting time. However, what is probably the case is that they have finally become painfully aware of just how much time they have actually been wasting in the past!

Music, television, noise, lighting too bright or too dim, temperature too high or too low, people talking, telephone	Choose your study location carefully. These should be eliminated by just choosing a proper spot.
Party or activity that you want to attend, family or friends wanting you to do something	If possible, plan your study session ahead of activity and use it as a reward.

Do the Concentration Worksheet to determine your specific problems.

WHY IS A "PLACE OF STUDY" SO IMPORTANT?

By looking at internal and external distractors, you can see how many can be controlled by the place you choose to study. It is important to have a definite and permanent place to study. Psychologists believe a conditioning effect is created between your desk and you. Do not do any other activities at your study desk. You should associate your study place with studying alone. Don't write letters, daydream, plan activities, or visit with friends in your study place. You need a study place where you feel comfortable and where you are likely to have few distractions.

HOW DO YOU IMPROVE CONCENTRATION WHILE READING?

Dr. Walter Pauk, noted study skills expert, believes the best way to gain and maintain concentration while you read is by having a lively conversation with the author. (No one will have to know!) Agree or disagree with the author. Interject your thoughts and ideas. This will also lead to more comprehension.

One reason your mind may wander during reading is because material is unfamiliar or too difficult. You cannot concentrate on what you can't comprehend. Formulate a purpose for reading! It also never hurts to look up words when you do not know the meanings!

WHAT ARE SOME STRATEGIES TO STRENGTHEN CONCENTRATION?

1. Learn to beat boredom—If boredom is causing a problem with concentration, study in small groups occasionally, buy review manuals and workbooks and look at the material from a different angle. Perhaps a tutor could provide new insights.

2. Become more active in studying—Highlight, underline, make questions out of the material, paraphrase, construct mnemonics, and/or form imagery associations. Think about your learning style and put it to work.

3. Ignore external distractions—A vibrating tuning fork held close to a spider's web sets up vibrations in the web. After the spider makes a few investigations and doesn't find dinner, it learns to ignore the vibrations. If a spider can control external distractors, a student should be able to eventually ignore external distractions.

MEMORY

Your brain is constantly being attacked with all kinds of information. You need to learn to process all of this by selective attention. Unimportant information signals are discarded immediately, such as a dog barking, a bird chirping, or the wind blowing. Other signals are only recalled for a moment. These signals will either be stored or dropped. As you are reading, you may recall the sentence you just finished. But, it may be difficult to recall that sentence when you finish a paragraph. The exact wording of that sentence has probably been dropped. If you can remember the concept of the sentence, you have probably stored that information in your memory.

It is important to note that without memory, there would be no learning.

Before you start reading this portion of the chapter, complete the Memory Worksheets.

What Are the Three Stages in the Memory Process?

1. Respond—If you don't understand material you are trying to remember, you don't have a chance to respond. One method we have of understanding new information is to relate it to what we already know. It will be helpful when starting a new chapter in a text to stop and think about what you already know about the material. What does this information mean to you before you learn anything new about it? To help you respond to information it is advantageous to use all of your senses: Listen to the lecture, take notes on it, and read about it.

2. Reserve—The key to reserving or retaining information is to make a conscious effort to remember. You need to find a reason to remember! One of the best ways to reserve information is to use or practice this information.

3. Remember—Our mind enables us to remember or recall information we have retained. Organization is an important factor in recall. Using your preferred learning style is also an asset. Review is vital for recalling information.

The immediate memory is called your short-term memory. This information is either discarded and forgotten or it is transferred into your permanent memory. This permanent memory is your long-term memory. Not all information stored in your long-term memory is in a form that can be retrieved. Short-term memory plays an important role in our everyday life. It is also vital in reading and study situations. The transfer of memory from short-term to long-term is enhanced by organization, repetition, and association with what we already know.

A study conducted at Southwest Missouri State University by Dr. Charles Tegeler revealed information on the value of review to help you remember. Students were given information and they studied it until they had 100 percent mastery. The group was divided into two groups. One group did not review the material and at the end of 63 days when they were retested, they averaged 17 percent comprehension. The other group reviewed once a week. At the end of the 63 day period, they averaged 92 percent comprehension! (See Figure 5.1.)

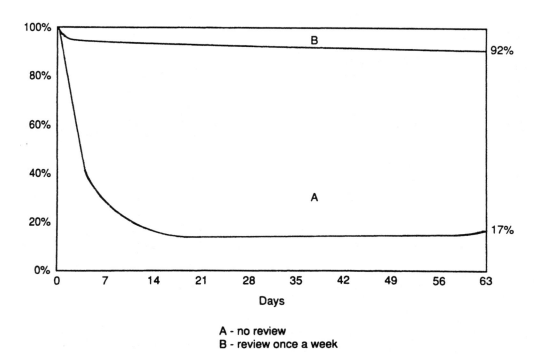

A - no review
B - review once a week

Figure 5.1

Why Do You Forget?

Forgetting can be defined as a failure or loss of memory. Your mind remembers only what you need and discards the rest. Do you remember grades you made in your classes in the eighth grade? Do you even remember what classes you had? You probably don't remember. Information that is not used is forgotten.

Research has proven over and over that the greatest amount of forgetting occurs during the first day. Remembering what you have heard is even more difficult to remember than what you have read. When you read, you have control over the material. You can slow down, regress, or speed-up your reading.

People often say they forgot something when they actually never knew it. If you just met someone and didn't really catch their name, you didn't forget it—you probably never knew it.

There are a variety of theories about forgetting. Think about these as you read them and see if you can understand how the theory relates to your own "forgetful" experiences.

1. It's There Somewhere!—Some psychologists believe once we have thoroughly learned something, it remains in our memory our entire life. This theory suggests that the concept is there, but we are just having trouble finding it in order to be able to retrieve it.

2. Interference Theory—Old facts and ideas cause us to forget new facts and ideas. The reverse is also true. New ideas and facts can cause confusion with old ones. We are continually adding ideas to our memory bank. If you learn three similar facts at three separate times, the middle one will have the most difficult time surviving. This is also true of lists you need to remember. The first and last items are easier to remember than the middle ones.

3. Use It or Lose It—If you don't use a fact you have learned, it gets more difficult to remember it. This is why review is so important!

4. Motivation and Attitude Theory—Here are our two favorite words again! Sometimes we choose to forget. Things we associate with unpleasant memories or mistakes we have made we would like to forget. A poor attitude in class can definitely affect memory ability. You have the power to influence both remembering and forgetting.

How Can You Enhance Your Memory?

Our most powerful attack against forgetting is cognitive processing. This simply means deep thinking. It is deep thinking that makes a long-lasting memory trace. According to Walter Pauk, there are three steps in cognitive processing or deep thinking:

1. Understand the fact thoroughly; be able to explain it in your own words.
2. Analyze the fact by viewing it from all sides.
3. Relate the fact to information you already have.

Using memory effectively is being able to recall information at the right time. Our memory system needs to be flexible.

The following ideas should help improve your memory:

1. *Organization*—The first step in organizing is to get a broad overview. Learn general concepts before you learn specifics. If you have a "feel" for the general idea, the details will have a place to fit.

   Research has shown that our short-term memory has a limited capacity. Seven unrelated items are about maximum for most people to remember. In various college classes, you will need to remember more than seven unrelated items. The way to handle this is through meaningful organization.

   Chunking or Clustering—This is a method whereby you categorize similar items you need to know. For example:

   As you walked to the grocery store, you realized you didn't have your list with you. You did remember there were twelve items. The items you had on your list were:

   onions, lettuce, ice cream, bananas, green beans, eggs, cheese, peas, apples, grapefruit, milk, and oranges.

   Look at these items for 15 seconds. Close the book and see how many you can recall. You are doing well if you remember 6 or 7.

   By clustering or chunking these items, we can make them manageable. We can have 3 major items instead of twelve.

VEGETABLES	DAIRY	FRUITS
onions	ice cream	bananas
lettuce	milk	apples
green beans	eggs	grapefruit
peas	cheese	oranges

When we think of the major headings, the individual details fall in place. The thought of dairy products automatically reduces our thoughts to dairy products. This procedure will work well in your textbooks. Learn to associate details with the major headings.

John Morris suggests a similar organizational technique. A good way to consolidate and summarize information you need to remember is to use the "poker-chip" strategy. In the game of poker, the blue chips are worth the most, followed by red chips and then the white chips. By analogy, the most important ideas in any message are the blue chips. Next to the blue chip ideas are the red chip, and subordinate to the red chip are the white chip ideas, which may be considered details.

Around a poker table, you'll usually find a player has many more white chips than red or blue. Usually he will also have a few more red chips than blue. A writer has few blue chip ideas, a few more red chip, and many more white chip ideas. When you are summarizing, mark white chip ideas with a W, the red chip ideas with an R, and the blue chip ideas with a B. This technique makes main ideas easy to remember. The main ideas act as magnets holding together the subordinate ideas and the supporting details.

2. *Visualize Relationships and Associations*—Knowing individual facts does not help you understand a topic. Relating details provides a basis for the main idea. Also, it is important to relate new ideas to what you already know. Visualizing uses a different part of your brain than when you just read. This will also aid in retention. Often students will remember a picture, table, or graph that explains a theory easier than they will remember the words that described it. The better our background, the easier this will be.

3. *Make It Meaningful*—We remember things better when we can apply them to ourselves. If we can match the information we need to remember to a goal we have set, it will be easier to recall.

4. *Intend to Remember*—Your mental attitude plays an important role in your memory. Intending to learn can create a positive attitude that will include other important characteristics, such as active learning, paying attention, and writing to understand.

5. *Motivated Interest*—Research has shown that interest is important to learning, but remembering is almost impossible without interest. If you are not interested in a class you are taking, find some way to create an interest. We tend to forget information that contradicts our opinions. If you feel bored, consider the possibility that you are creating your boredom. Take responsibility for your attitudes.

6. *Recitation*—This technique is probably the most powerful one that will allow transfer from short-term to long-term memory. When you want to remember

something, repeat it aloud. Recitation works best when you put concepts you want to remember into your own words.

Arthur Gates did a series of recitation experiments in 1917. His experiments suggest that when you are reading a general text (psychology, sociology, history), 80 percent of your time should be spent in reciting and 20 percent in reading. It is also more effective to start recitation early in the reading process. Do not wait until you have read everything before you start to recite.

7. *Spaced Study*—Marathon study sessions are not effective. It is much better to have intermittent spaced review sessions. A practical application of this would be using the small blocks of time you are now wasting during the day. It is also important to take breaks while you are studying. After 45–50 minutes, reward yourself with a short break. When you come back, you will be more alert and more efficient. If significant learning is taking place and you are really engrossed, go for it! You don't have to stop, but memory is more productive when you space your studying instead of trying to accomplish everything in one long session.

8. *Brainstorming*—If you are having a problem recalling an answer on a test, try brainstorming. Think of everything you can that is related to what you are trying to remember. For example, if you are trying to remember your fifth grade teacher's name, think of other elementary teachers you had. By association the name you are trying to remember should pop up during this brainstorming.

9. *Reflecting*—It is important to give information time to go from short-term memory to long-term memory. This is considered consolidation time. Researchers vary on their opinions, but a safe rule is to leave information in your short-term memory 4–15 seconds. This gives information time to consolidate and transfer to your long-term memory. This is important to remember when you are reading quickly and not stopping to think about what you have read. The information will be discarded quickly if you do not allow time for transfer. Stop and think about what you have just read, recite it, paraphrase it, and relate it to what you already know.

10. *Use All Your Senses*—The more senses you involve in studying, the better your memory process will work. Read and visualize, recite key concepts, devise questions, and write answers.

11. *Combine Memory Techniques*—You can combine organizing, reciting, and reflecting in one task. Different techniques can reinforce each other.

12. *Repetition*—Simply repeating things will aid memory. Advertisements hook us in this way. We learn a jingle by hearing it repeated again and again. For example:

    "You Deserve a Break Today" . . . McDonalds

    "It's the Real Thing" . . . Coke

    "Ring around the Collar" . . . Wisk Detergent

    "You've Got the Right One, Baby" . . . Diet Pepsi

13. *Mnemonics*—Mnemonics are easily remembered words, rhymes, phrases, sentences, or games that help you remember difficult lists, principles, or facts.

    An example of a rhyming association could be:

    "In fourteen hundred and ninety-two Columbus sailed the ocean blue."

If you have a group to remember or a list of items, you can make-a-word mnemonic. An easy way to remember the Great Lakes is by the word HOMES—Huron, Ontario, Michigan, Erie, and Superior.

Similar to this is an acronym. An acronym is formed by the first letters of the words you want to remember. A good example of this would be the note taking system introduced in this text.

> *TRQ: Take notes*
> *Revise notes*
> *Question main points*

Another mnemonic device is to make a sentence you can remember. You make the sentence using words you devised from the first letter of the words you need to remember. For example:

> You need to remember the factors that are involved in the quality of your sleep. These factors are the habit of your sleep, the environment where you sleep, the duration, your general health, and the use of drugs.

Your mnemonic sentence could be: "Hey everyone, don't have drugs."

You made these words using key words in the list you needed to remember:

> *Hey—habit*
> *everyone—environment*
> *don't—duration*
> *have—health*
> *drugs—drugs*

It is important to note that mnemonics do not help you understand the material. They assist in rote memorization.

GENERAL STUDY SKILLS

The next section is to make you think of different areas in general study skills. Answer the questions honestly and, after each major section, write a brief paragraph describing your habits in these areas and whether they are potential problems. Awareness of the problems in these different areas is the beginning of more efficient study.

SUMMARY

The best way to improve your concentration is by identifying and eliminating internal and external distractors. You are in control of internal distractors. External distractors may be beyond your control, but you can learn to control your reactions to them. A proper place to study and how you study also affect concentration. Take frequent breaks and reward yourself!

Recall ability is controlled by your memory processes. Forgetting occurs very rapidly unless you take certain steps to prevent this. Realizing the importance of organization, visualization, intention to remember, interest, recitation, combining memory techniques, spaced study, brainstorming, reflecting, using your senses, and mnemonics will help you in strengthening your recall ability.

NAME: _____ **DATE:** _____

EXERCISE 1. CONCENTRATION WORKSHEET

During your next study session, keep a record of internal and external distractors. On the chart below, write what the distractor was. After your study session, determine whether the distractor was internal or external. Write a brief solution.

DISTRACTION	EXTERNAL/INTERNAL	SOLUTION
1. _____		
2. _____		
3. _____		
4. _____		
5. _____		
6. _____		
7. _____		
8. _____		
9. _____		
10. _____		

When considering the solutions—how many do you feel you can control? Write a brief paragraph explaining how you can possibly prevent these distractions.

_____

_____

_____

_____

_____

_____

_____

_____

_____

_____

_____

_____

_____

_____

_____

_____

_____

_____

_____

_____

_____

_____

_____

_____

_____

_____

_____

_____

NAME: _____ **DATE:** _____

EXERCISE 2. MEMORY WORKSHEET

List five things easy to remember.

1. _____

2. _____

3. _____

4. _____

5. _____

List five things difficult to remember.

1. _____

2. _____

3. _____

4. _____

5. _____

Name three reasons there is a difference between these two lists.

1. _____

_____

2. _____

_____

3. _____

_____

NAME: _____ **DATE:** _____

EXERCISE 3. YOUR MEMORY HABITS

Answer yes or no to the following questions:

		YES	NO
1.	Do you intend to remember your course work?	_____	_____
2.	Do you try to get interested in your classes?	_____	_____
3.	Do you honestly focus your full attention while studying?	_____	_____
4.	Do you review lecture and textbook notes once a week or more?	_____	_____
5.	Do you use organization in your study sessions?	_____	_____
6.	Do you study in short spaced (45–50 minutes) sessions with breaks?	_____	_____
7.	Do you keep an open mind when being introduced to new material?	_____	_____
8.	Do you recite material you are trying to remember?	_____	_____
9.	Do you make an effort to understand the material, not just read it?	_____	_____
10.	Do you use several methods to reinforce memory, i.e., reciting, discussing with friends, and effective note taking?	_____	_____

If you answer yes to 7 or more of these, you are on the right track! If you have 3 or more no answers, you need to evaluate your study habits.

Write a brief paragraph explaining what you intend to start doing to develop your memory.

_____

_____

_____

_____

_____

_____

_____

_____

EXERCISE 4. WORK AND STUDY HABITS

	YES	NO
1. Do I study alone?	_____	_____
2. Do I listen to the radio or TV while I study?	_____	_____
3. Do I plan my study time so that I can finish what I start?	_____	_____
4. Do I prepare for exams?	_____	_____
5. Am I flustered by exams?	_____	_____
6. Are my study periods interrupted by family or friends?	_____	_____
7. Does illness interfere with my studying?	_____	_____
8. Do I smoke while I study?	_____	_____
9. Is my work of an inferior quality?	_____	_____
10. Do I feel that I am accomplishing anything when I study?	_____	_____

Evaluate your work and study habits:

_____

_____

_____

_____

_____

_____

_____

_____

_____

_____

_____

_____

_____

NAME: _____ **DATE:** _____

EXERCISE 5. NOTE TAKING HABITS

		YES	NO
1.	Do I try to write down everything the instructor says in class?	_____	_____
2.	Do I take more notes only on those things which interest me?	_____	_____
3.	Are my notes meaningless after I leave the class?	_____	_____
4.	Do I put my notes in good order soon after writing them in class?	_____	_____
5.	Do I feel too much pressure in class to take notes effectively?	_____	_____
6.	Do I have difficulty taking notes and keeping up with the lecture?	_____	_____
7.	Has note taking been very helpful in the past?	_____	_____
8.	Am I able to pick out the important points in lectures?	_____	_____
9.	Is my background so weak I cannot make sense from the lecture to write effective notes?	_____	_____
10.	Do my feelings about some of the instructors make it difficult to take notes?	_____	_____

My Problems:

_____

_____

_____

_____

_____

_____

_____

_____

_____

_____

_____

NAME: _____ DATE: _____

EXERCISE 6. READING AND THINKING HABITS

		YES	NO
1.	Do I like to read fiction?	_____	_____
2.	Do I read books not related to classwork?	_____	_____
3.	Do I formulate questions during reading?	_____	_____
4.	Do I read newspapers and magazines?	_____	_____
5.	Do I read too slowly?	_____	_____
6.	Does my mind wander when I read?	_____	_____
7.	Do I daydream in class?	_____	_____
8.	When I read something long, do I finish?	_____	_____
9.	Is my best reading done at a certain time of day or night?	_____	_____
10.	Do I read word-for-word?	_____	_____
11.	Do I preview the material before reading?	_____	_____
12.	Does the mood I'm in play an important role in my reading?	_____	_____
13.	Does my weak vocabulary cause me to read slowly?	_____	_____
14.	Do I read for leisure?	_____	_____

Evaluate your reading and thinking skills:

_____

_____

_____

_____

_____

_____

_____

_____

_____

NAME: _____ DATE: _____

EXERCISE 7. LEISURE-TIME HABITS

		YES	NO
1.	Do I participate in physical activities (in school or out)?	_____	_____
2.	Do I like to work with a hobby?	_____	_____
3.	Do I loaf with my friends when I should be studying?	_____	_____
4.	Do I "try to get away" occasionally in order to think?	_____	_____
5.	Am I bored when I am at home?	_____	_____
6.	Am I fatigued long before bedtime?	_____	_____
7.	Do I work for pay when I am not in school?	_____	_____
8.	Do my family obligations take the place of studying?	_____	_____
9.	Am I unable to schedule time for family and friends?	_____	_____
10.	When I do get leisure time, I am not able to enjoy it because of stress of guilt feelings about not spending enough time with my family.	_____	_____

My Problems:

_____

_____

_____

_____

_____

_____

_____

_____

_____

_____

Chapter 6

Test Taking

For effective students, testing is more than dumping material. It is more than the end point of a grading period. The actual act of taking an exam is only one step in the learning process. Advance preparation for exams is critical. Likewise, intelligent performance during an exam will often make the difference between success and failure.

PREPARING FOR EXAMS

There are many types and purposes of college examinations. They range from the frequent short quiz through the hour exam, mid-term, and final exam. The method of preparation for each exam must be adapted to the type and purpose of the exam. A wise student starts preparing for finals the first day of classes. No amount of cramming during the final week will make up for lack of study during the semester. Careful preparation of assignments removes the necessity for the frenzied type of last minute work in which many students indulge, but does not remove the necessity for intensive review before an exam.

> *Systematic review is effective review.*

During the week or 10 days preceding final exams, a definite schedule should be set up so that all material will be covered in several sessions rather than in one long session. In reviews, just as in other types of study, short sessions are much more profitable than long drawn out cramming sessions. Reviews should be directed at integrating knowledge, since isolated facts are difficult to remember, and often meaningless. Relating your collection of facts to the major points in the course will make it much easier to remember them and make them more useful. The following is a suggested procedure for test review.

OBJECTIVE EXAMS

Multiple choice, matching, true-false, and completion exams are considered to be objective exams. They usually have one specific answer and little variation in the answer is accepted. Some specific tips to taking objective exams are listed below. Of course none of these suggestions are more important than solid advance preparation. However, once you feel you have done all you can to prepare for an exam, a certain degree of "test-wiseness" is valuable.

From Academic Effectiveness: A Manual for Scholastic Success at the United States Naval Academy, Fourth Edition *by The United States Naval Academy. © 1996 by Eric D. Bowman. Used with permission.*

Taking Objective Exams

1. When reporting for an examination, pay very close attention the whole time you are there. Listen very closely to all directions. Ask questions if you are in doubt. Be absolutely certain of what is expected of you. Find out if there is a penalty for guessing. Are incorrect answers weighted more than correct ones?

2. Find out exactly how much time you have and try to estimate the amount of time per question or per five questions.

3. *Read closely* and pay attention. Reading directions and listening to verbal comments about the directions are vital to answering correctly.

4. While objective exams often do not allow enough time for you to read through the whole exam twice, at least glance through it to find any sections that might be more time consuming. *Plan your time accordingly.*

5. Put off answering the more difficult or questionable items. Mark the ones you skip in the margin. Be sure and remember to return to these items before you turn in your exam.

6. Read all five choices, even when an early one seems to be the logical answer. Sometimes the fifth choice says: "All of the above," or "Two of the above," and you may only be partially correct by taking the first choice.

7. If there are five choices, read each one and cross out the choices you know to be definitely wrong. If in doubt, this narrows down the field and you stand a better chance of guessing right among two or three answers than among five.

8. Remember—almost everyone is going to miss questions. If you can avoid getting jittery over a number of missed answers and go on with a confident attitude, you will come out on top. Do not blow the exam by imagining that all is lost just because you missed what seems like a large number.

9. *Do not panic* if you see someone moving along faster than you are. If someone leaves early, he or she may have given up. Often the exams are constructed to last longer than the time given.

10. After you have left the exam room, have a debriefing with yourself. Jot down the topics covered in the exam, noting the sections of your textbooks that were covered. Note the strengths and weaknesses of your exam preparation.

11. Plan ahead to do better next time, especially in eliminating the kinds of mistakes that seem to have caused you some loss.

There are also ways to improve your performance on multiple-choice exams when your only alternative is guessing. The following suggestions are useful when all else fails.

When Studying Isn't Enough

1. You must select not only a technically correct answer, but the most *completely correct answer.* Since "all of the above" and "none of the above" are very inclusive statements, these options tend to be correct more often than would be predicted by chance alone.

1. MAJOR TOPICS

Make a list of the major topics in the course. Skim assignment sheets, lecture notes, outlines of outside reading and quiz papers so you are sure that the list is complete.

2. SUMMARY

Write a summary or outline of related material for each of the major topics. Place particular emphasis on relationships among the topics.

3. SYSTEMATIC REVIEW

Go over the materials systematically. Apply more of your time to the subject in most need of work.

4. MOCK EXAM

Make out a set of probable questions. Keep in mind what you know about your professor's interests and points of importance. Using this mock exam is an excellent way to review after all the material has been covered.

5. REST

Adequate rest is essential. It is impossible to think clearly after an all night session of cramming. Many students find themselves unable to recall information which they had previously mastered. If at all possible, an early bedtime (before midnight) is critical for effective test performance.

6. RELAX!

Many students face every exam with such an emotional reaction that they find it impossible to demonstrate their knowledge. Avoiding last minute discussions is extremely important if you feel that excess anxiety interferes with your ability to perform. During exam week it is also wise to avoid post-exam discussions which may only give you a feeling of failure to take to the next exam.

2. *Be wary of options which include unqualified absolutes* such as "never," "always," "are," "guarantees," "insures." Such statements are highly restrictive and very difficult to defend. They are rarely (though they may sometimes be) correct options.

3. The less frequently stated converse of the above is that carefully qualified, conservative, or *"guarded" statements tend to be correct* more often than would be predicted by chance alone. Other things being equal, choose options containing such qualifying phrases as "may sometimes be," or "can occasionally result in."

4. Watch out for extra-long options or those with a lot of jargon. These are frequently used as decoys.

5. Use your knowledge of common prefixes, suffixes and root words to make intelligent guesses about terminology that you don't know. A knowledge of the prefix

"hyper," for instance, would clue you that hypertension refers to high, not low blood pressure.

6. *Be alert to grammatical construction.* The correct answer to an item stem which ends in "an" would obviously be an option starting with a vowel. Watch also for agreement of subjects and verbs.

7. Utilize information and insights that you've acquired in working through the entire test to go back and answer earlier items of which you weren't sure.

8. If you have absolutely *NO* idea what the answer is, can't use any of the above techniques and there is no scoring penalty for guessing, choose option B or C. Studies indicate that these are correct slightly more often than would be predicted by chance alone.

ESSAY EXAMS

In general, essay questions are aimed at revealing your ability to make and support valid generalizations, or to apply broad principles to a series of specific instances. The question will be directed toward some major thought area. For example, in a literature course you might be asked to contrast two authors' implicit opinions about the nature of mankind. In an American History course you might be asked to discuss Madison's ideas on control of fraction, as reflected in the organization of the legislature of the United States.

Short essay questions are more apt to be aimed at your ability to produce and present accurate explanations, backed by facts. A sample short question in a literature course might be: "In a well-organized paragraph, explain Poe's theory of poetry." In a history course you might be asked to list the major provisions of a treaty, and explain briefly the significance of each provision.

Preparing for Essay Exams

1. Preparation for an essay exam, as for any exam, requires close and careful rereading and review of text and lecture notes. The emphasis in this kind of an exam is on thought areas.

2. It is often possible to find out what exam format the professor usually uses; a series of short answer types, one long essay, etc. You should ask the professor what exam format should be expected. This is not the same as asking what specific questions will be on the exam. In fact, many professors announce in advance the general areas the exam will cover—concepts, issues, controversies, theories, rival interpretations, or whatever.

3. Reviewing your lecture notes will also reveal which broad areas have been central to class discussion. Begin by asking yourself about the main concepts and relationships involved in the material you are reviewing. Review your notes with a broad view. Don't worry about detail at first. Review major headings and chapter summaries in your textbooks. Boil your material down to a tight outline form.

4. Once you have the main concepts organized in a thoughtful pattern, fill in the necessary details. On an essay exam you will be facing the task of arriving at a sound generalization and then proving it through the skillful use of detail. You

must therefore have the details at your command. But remember, no detail is crucial. Select the details that best go to prove a concept.

5. Some students profit by making up sample questions and then practicing answering them. In a history course for instance you might test yourself by answering questions such as "Explain what John C. Calhoun meant by the term concurrent majority and compare his ideas to Jefferson's on majority rule."

6. Part of the groundwork for all exams is mastering the terminology used in the course. Getting this out of the way is critical.

Taking Essay Exams

1. When you first get the exam, look for the point value of each question. If the questions are not weighted equally, you need to decide how much time to spend on each question. Adjust your timing so that you allow longer time for longer answers. If necessary, borrow time from the short answers. If the point value is not listed, you have a right to ask if all questions have equal value.

2. Read the directions and each question carefully. Try to understand exactly what is asked. Glance rapidly over all the questions before you start putting down your answers. An essay question always has a controlling idea expressed in one or two words. Find the key words and underline them.

3. As you skim over the test, note down key words or phrases for each question. This will serve to stimulate other ideas. Make the initial sentence of your answer the best possible one sentence answer to the entire question. Then elaborate in subsequent sentences. As ideas about other questions occur to you, immediately jot them down on scratch paper before they slip away.

4. Think through your answer before you start to write it. Use scratch paper for outlining if necessary. A little time spent on a brief outline pays big dividends for the few seconds spent. A planned answer saves you from a lot of excess words which are time consuming but worth little. If the question seems ambiguous, vague, or too broad, make clear your interpretation of the question before attempting to answer it.

5. Take care to write legibly, leave adequate margins and space your work attractively. Use good English and remember that neat papers tend to be scored higher.

6. Usually professors do not want your answer to cover everything you have learned in the course. Your essay answers should be organized, concise, to the point and with only those details needed to fill out a full picture. Do not try to reproduce the whole book. If supporting evidence is asked for, add as many details as possible.

7. Star or underline important ideas appearing late in the material. If information you have given in answer to one question ties into another, point out the interrelation. It may be worth credit.

8. Check off each question as you answer it to avoid omitting one. Reread each answer before proceeding to the next in order to correct errors or omissions.

9. Try to budget time so that you have time to proof read your answers before you turn in the exam.

10. *Use all the time allotted to you!*

Chapter 7

Liberal Arts

The Meaning and Purpose of General Education

REFLECTION 7.1

Before you start reading this chapter, do your best to answer the question below. **Note:** This is not a test. (Repeat: This is not a test.)

Which one of the following statements do you think represents the most accurate meaning of the term *liberal arts*?

1. Learning to be less politically conservative.
2. Learning to be more artistic.
3. Learning about ideas rather than acquiring practical skills.
4. Learning to spend money freely.
5. Learning skills for freedom.

(You will find the answer to this question later in the chapter.)

WHAT IS THE *MEANING* AND *PURPOSE* OF THE LIBERAL ARTS?

If you're uncertain about what the term "liberal arts" means, you're not alone. Most first-year students don't have a clear idea about what the liberal arts actually represent (73). If they were to guess, they might mistakenly say that it's something "impractical" or, perhaps, something to do with liberal politics—as illustrated by the following experience.

PERSONAL EXPERIENCE BY JOE CUSEO

I was once advising a first-year student who intended to major in business. While helping her plan the courses she needed to complete her degree, I pointed out to her that she still needed to take a course in philosophy. After I made this point, here's how our conversation went.

Student (in a somewhat irritated tone): "Why do I have to take philosophy? I'm a business major."

Dr. Cuseo: "Because philosophy is an important component of a liberal arts education."

Student (in a very agitated tone): "I'm not liberal and I don't want to be a liberal. I'm conservative and so are my parents; we all voted for Ronald Reagan last election!"

"Knowledge will forever govern ignorance; and a people who mean to be their own governors must arm themselves with the power which knowledge gives."

–James Madison, fourth president of the United States and co-signer of the American Constitution and Bill of Rights

"It is such good fortune for people in power that people do not think."

–Adolf Hitler, German dictator

"In a nation whose citizens are to be led by persuasion and not by force, the art of reasoning becomes of the first importance."

–Thomas Jefferson, third president of the United States and primary author of the Declaration of Independence

The student probably would have picked choice "1" as her answer to the multiple-choice question posed at the start of this chapter. (She would have been wrong because option "5" is the correct answer.) Literally translated, the term "liberal arts" derives from the Latin words "liberales"—meaning to *liberate* or *free*, and "artes"—meaning *skills*. Thus, "skills for freedom" is the most accurate meaning of the term "liberal arts."

The roots of the "liberal arts" date back to the origin of modern civilization—to the ancient Greeks and Romans—who advocated for a democratic government in which the people choose (elect) their own leaders. In a democracy or free society, people should be *liberated* from uncritical dependence on a dictator or autocrat. To preserve political freedom and engage effectively in self-governance, citizens in a democracy needed to be well-educated, critical thinkers capable of making wise choices about whom they elect as their leaders and lawmakers (11, 19).

The political ideals of the ancient Greeks and Romans were shared by the founding fathers of the United States who also emphasized the importance of an educated citizenry for preserving America's new democracy. As Thomas Jefferson, third president of the United States, wrote in 1801:

> "I know of no safe depository of the ultimate powers of a society but the people themselves; and if we think them not enlightened enough to exercise control with a wholesome discretion [responsible decision-making], the remedy is not to take power from them, but to inform their discretion by education." (40).

Thus, the origins of liberal arts are rooted in the democratic ideal that education is essential for preserving political freedom. Citizens educated in the liberal arts acquire the breadth of knowledge and depth of thinking needed to vote wisely, preserve democracy, and oppose autocracy (dictatorship). In other words, citizens must learn to think for themselves rather than have someone else (a dictator) do their thinking for them.

The importance of a knowledgeable, critical-thinking citizenry for preserving democracy remains relevant today. Contemporary political campaigns make frequent use of manipulative media advertisements that rely on short sound bites, one-sided arguments, and powerful visual images, which are intentionally designed to appeal to voters' emotions rather than their reasoning skills (65).

Over time, the term "liberal arts" acquired the additional meaning of liberating (freeing) people to be *self-directed* individuals who make choices and decisions guided by their own, well-informed ideas and personal values rather than by blind conformity to the ideas and values of others (162). Self-directed human beings are liberated not only from manipulation and control by political figures, but also from:

- Any authority figure—e.g., they question and challenge excessive use or abuse of authority by parents, teachers, or law enforcers;

- Peers—e.g., they resist irrational or unethical peer pressure; and

- Media—e.g., they detect and reject forms of advertisements designed to manipulate their self-image or material needs.

THE LIBERAL ARTS CURRICULUM

Based on this educational philosophy of the ancient Greeks and Romans, the first liberal arts curriculum (collection of courses) was developed during the Middle Ages and consisted of seven courses divided into two general areas: (a) the trivium (a set of three courses): logic, grammar, and rhetoric—the art of oral argumentation and persuasion, and (b) the quadrivium (a set of four courses): music, arithmetic, geometry, and astronomy (134). The original liberal arts curriculum reflected the belief that individuals who experienced these courses would acquire (a) a *broad* base of knowledge that left them well informed in a variety of different subjects and (b) a complete set of mental skills that enabled them to think *deeply* and *critically*.

The purpose of the original liberal arts curriculum has withstood the test of time. Today's colleges and universities continue to offer a liberal arts curriculum designed to provide students with a broad base of knowledge in multiple subject areas that equips them with critical thinking skills. The liberal arts curriculum today is sometimes called *general education*—to represent the fact that it leads to knowledge and skills that are "general" or flexible, rather than rigid or narrowly specialized. General education signifies what *all* college graduates learn in common—i.e., what every college graduate should know and be able to do, regardless of their specific major or specialized field may be (10). On some campuses, the liberal arts are also referred to as:

1. **The core curriculum:** "Core" standing for what is central or essential for effective performance in any field; or
2. **Breadth requirements:** Referring to the fact that they embrace a wide range of subject areas designed to provide a broad base of knowledge and skills.

REFLECTION 7.2

To be successful in any major or career, what do you think a person should:

1. Know?
2. Be able to do?

> Whatever term is used on your campus to describe the liberal arts, the bottom line is that they provide the foundational component of a college education upon which all academic specializations (majors) are built.; they embody what all college students graduates should be able to *know* and *do* for whatever occupational path they choose to pursue; they distinguish a college education from vocational preparation, and they define what it means to be a well-rounded and well-educated person.

SUBJECT AREAS (DIVISIONS OF KNOWLEDGE) IN THE LIBERAL ARTS CURRICULUM

On average, about twelve to fourteen courses, or about one-third of a college graduate's course credits, are required general education courses taken from the liberal arts curriculum (39). The subject areas in the contemporary liberal arts curriculum have expanded well beyond the seven courses that comprised the original curriculum at medieval universities. The *divisions* of knowledge that comprise the liberal arts today, and the *courses* that make up each division, vary somewhat from campus to campus. Campuses also vary in terms of the nature and number of required courses within each division of knowledge, as well as the range or variety of course choices that students may choose from to fulfill their general education requirements.

Despite campus-to-campus variation in the number and nature of courses required, the liberal arts curriculum on every campus represents the areas of knowledge and the types of skills that all college graduates should possess. Listed below are the general divisions of knowledge and related subject areas that comprise the liberal arts curriculum on most campuses today. As you read the following divisions of knowledge, highlight any subject areas in which you have never had a course.

Humanities

Courses in this division of the liberal arts curriculum focus on the *human experience* and *human culture*. They ask the "big questions" that arise in the life of all human beings, such as: Why are we here? What is the meaning or purpose of our existence? How should I live? What is the good life? Is there life after death? Courses in this branch of the liberal arts are also designed to develop those skills that relate specifically to human language, such as reading, writing, and speaking.

Primary Subject Areas

> "For me, (religious studies) is where I found meaning. How I value the liberal arts is in studying what it means to be human."
>
> —College senior and student body president (158)

- **English composition:** Writing clearly, critically, and persuasively.
- **Speech:** Speaking eloquently and persuasively.
- **Literature:** Reading critically and appreciating the artistic merit of various literary genres (forms of writing), such as novels, short stories, poems, plays, and essays.
- **Foreign languages:** Listening, speaking, reading, and writing in languages other than one's native tongue.

- **Philosophy:** Thinking rationally, developing wisdom (the ability to use knowledge prudently), and living an ethically principled life.

- **Religious studies:** Understanding how humans conceive of and express their faith in a transcendent (supreme) being.

- **History:** Understanding past events, their causes, their influence on current events, and their implications for future events. (**Note:** Some campuses classify history in the social sciences rather than the humanities.)

Fine Arts

Courses in this division of the liberal arts curriculum focus largely on the *artistic expression*, asking such questions as: How do humans create, demonstrate, and appreciate what is beautiful? How do humans express themselves aesthetically (through the senses) with imagination, originality, style, and elegance?

Primary Subject Areas

- **Visual arts:** Creating and appreciating human expression through visual representation (drawing, painting, sculpture, photography, and graphic design).

- **Musical arts:** Appreciating and creating rhythmical arrangements of sounds.

- **Performing arts:** Appreciating and expressing creativity through drama and dance.

Mathematics

Courses in this division of the liberal arts curriculum are designed to promote skills in *numerical* calculation, *quantitative* reasoning, and problem solving.

Primary Subject Areas

- **Algebra:** Mathematical reasoning through symbolic representation of numbers in a language of letters that vary in size or quantity.

- **Statistics:** Mathematical methods for summarizing, estimating probabilities, representing and understanding numerical information depicted in graphs, charts, and tables, and drawing accurate conclusions from quantitative data.

- **Calculus:** Higher mathematical methods for calculating the rate at which the quantity of one entity changes in relation to another and mathematical methods for measuring areas enclosed by curves.

Natural Sciences

Courses in this division of the liberal arts curriculum are devoted to systematic observation of the *physical world* and explanation of *natural phenomena*. They ask such questions as: What causes the physical events that take place in the natural world? How can we predict and control these events? How do we promote a symbiotic relationship between the human world and the natural (physical) environment that serves to sustain the survival of both?

> "Dancing is silent poetry."
> —Simonides, ancient Greek poet

> "The universe is a grand book which cannot be read until one learns to comprehend the language and become familiar with the characters of which it is composed. It is written in the language of mathematics."
> —Galileo Galilei, a.k.a., Galileo, -seventeenth century Italian physicist, mathematician, astronomer, and philosopher

> "Science is an imaginative adventure of the mind seeking truth in a world of mystery."
> —Sir Cyril Herman Hinshelwood, Nobel Prize-winning English chemist

Primary Subject Areas

- **Biology:** Understanding the structure and underlying processes of all living things.
- **Chemistry:** Understanding the composition of natural and synthetic (man-made) substances and how these substances may be changed or developed.
- **Physics:** Understanding the properties of physical matter and the principles of energy, motion, and electrical and magnetic forces.
- **Geology:** Understanding the composition of the earth and the natural processes that have shaped its development.
- **Astronomy:** Understanding the composition and motion of celestial bodies that comprise the universe.

Social and Behavioral Sciences

Courses in this division of the liberal arts curriculum focus on the observation of *human behavior*, both individually and in groups, asking such questions as: What causes humans to behave the way they do? How can we predict, control, or improve human behavior and interpersonal interaction?

Primary Subject Areas

- **Psychology:** Understanding the human mind, its conscious and subconscious processes, and the underlying causes of human behavior.
- **Sociology:** Understanding the structure, interaction, and collective behavior of organized social groups, institutions, or systems that comprise human society (e.g., family, education, religion, criminal justice, and social services).
- **Anthropology:** Understanding the cultural and physical origin, development and distribution of the human species.
- **History:** Understanding past events, their causes, their influence on current events, and their implications for future events. (**Note:** Some campuses classify history in the humanities rather than social sciences.)
- **Political Science:** Understanding how societal authority is organized and how this authority is exerted to govern people, make collective decisions, and maintain social order.
- **Economics:** Understanding how the monetary needs of humans are met through the allocation of limited resources, and how material wealth is produced and distributed.
- **Geography:** Understanding how the place (physical location) where humans live influences their cultural and societal development, and how humans influence and are influenced by their surrounding physical environment.

Physical Education and Wellness

Courses in this division of the liberal arts curriculum focus on the *human body*—how to maintain optimal health and attain peak levels of performance—by asking such questions as: How does the body function most effectively? What can humans do to prevent illness, promote wellness, and improve the physical and mental quality of one's life?

> "Man, the molecule of society, is the subject of social science."
>
> —Henry Charles Carey, leading -nineteenth century American economist

> "To eat is a necessity, but to eat intelligently is an art."
>
> —La Rochefoucauld, -seventeenth century French author

Primary Subject Areas

- **Physical education:** Understanding the role of human exercise for promoting health and peak performance.

- **Nutrition:** Understanding how the body makes use of food and uses it as nourishment to promote health and generate energy.

- **Sexuality:** Understanding the biological, psychological, and social aspects of sexual relations.

- **Drug education:** Understanding how substances (chemicals) that alter the body and mind affect physical health, mental health, and human performance.

REFLECTION 7.3

Look back at the liberal arts' subject areas in which you have never had a course, and identify which of these areas strike you as particularly interesting or potentially useful. Provide a brief explanation why.

Most of your liberal arts requirements will be taken during your first two years of college. Don't be surprised or discouraged to find that some of these requirements sound similar to courses you had in high school. Don't begin to think that you will be bored to tears because you know all there is to know about these fields of study. College courses in the same subject areas that you may have experienced in high school will not be videotape replays of what you have already learned. You will move beyond basic competency in these subjects to more advanced levels of proficiency. You will delve more deeply into these subjects, learn about them in greater depth, and think about them at a higher level (39). In fact, research indicates that most of the gains in thinking that students make in college take place during their first two years—the very years in which they are taking most of their liberal arts courses (127).

The breadth of knowledge you acquire in the liberal arts allows you to stand on the shoulders of intellectual giants from a wide range of fields and capitalize on their collective wisdom. Also, keep in mind that the liberal arts do not just enable you to acquire a broad base of knowledge; they also discipline your mind to *think* in a wide variety of ways. This is why different academic subjects are often referred to as *disciplines*—by learning them, you begin to develop the "mental discipline" that faculty in these fields have spent years of their lives developing. For instance, when you study history, algebra, biology, and art, you are disciplining your mind to think chronologically (history), symbolically (algebra), scientifically (biology), and creatively (art). The diverse subjects in different divisions of the liberal arts will promote your mental flexibility by stretching your mind to think in a wide variety of ways, which include thinking:

- In the form of words, numbers, and images,

- In terms of specific parts and whole patterns,

- Locally and globally,
- Concretely and abstractly,
- Systematically (in sequential steps) and intuitively (in sudden leaps),
- Factually and imaginatively, and
- Objectively, subjectively, and symbolically (49, 78).

THE LIBERAL ARTS "LIBERATES" YOU FROM NARROWNESS BY BROADENING YOUR PERSPECTIVE OF THE WORLD AROUND YOU

The liberal arts provide you with a broad base of knowledge by exposing you to diverse fields of study. This breadth of knowledge will widen your perspective on the world around you (26). The key components of this broader perspective are organized and illustrated in the following figure.

In **Figure 7.1**, the center circle represents the **self**. Fanning out to the right of the self is a series of arches that encompass the **social-spatial perspective**, which includes increasingly larger social groups and more distant places—ranging from the narrowest perspective (the individual)—to the widest perspective (the universe). The liberal arts liberate you from the narrow "tunnel vision" of a self-centered (egocentric) perspective; it provides a panoramic perspective of the world that empowers you to step outside yourself and see yourself in relation to other people and other places.

In **Figure 7.1**, to the left of the self are three arches labeled the chronological perspective, which represent the three key dimensions of time: past (historical), present (contemporary), and future (futuristic). The liberal arts not only widen your perspective, they also lengthen it by stretching your vision beyond the present—enabling you to see yourself in relation to humans who have lived before us and who will live after us. The chronological perspective gives you hindsight to see where the world has been, insight into the world's current condition, and foresight to see where the world is going.

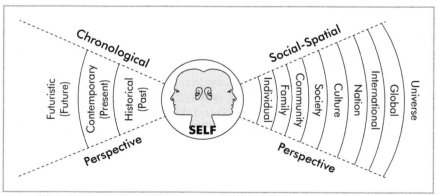

Figure 7.1. Multiple Perspectives Developed by the Liberal Arts.

It could be said that the chronological perspective provides you with a mental "time machine" that allows you to flash back to the past and flash forward to the future, while the *social-spatial* perspective provides you with a conceptual telescope that enables you to view people and places that are far away. These two broadening perspectives developed by the liberal arts combine to expand your perspective beyond the here and now, enabling you to view and appreciate the experiences of different people living in different places at different times.

Specific elements that comprise each of these broadening perspectives of the liberal arts are described below.

ELEMENTS OF THE SOCIAL-SPATIAL PERSPECTIVE: DIFFERENT PERSONS AND PLACES

The Perspective of Family

Moving beyond the perspective of yourself as an individual, you are part of a larger social unit—your *family*. Members of your family have undoubtedly influenced the person you are today and how you got to be that way. Moreover, your family has not only influenced you; you have influenced your family. For example, your decision to go to college has likely elevated your family's sense of pride and may influence other family members' decision to attend college. In addition, if or when you have children, your graduation from college will influence their future welfare. As will be mentioned children of college graduates experience improved intellectual development, better physical health, and greater economic security (24, 25, 126, 127).

The Perspective of Community

Moving beyond the family, you are also a member of a larger social unit—your *community*. This wider social circle includes friends and neighbors at home, at school, and at work. These are the communities in which you can begin to take action to improve the human condition. If you want to make the world a better place, this is the place to start—through civic engagement in your local communities.

Civic-minded and civically responsible step beyond their narrow self-interests and selflessly share their time or resources to help members of their community, particularly those in need. They demonstrate their humanity by being *humane*—i.e., showing genuine compassion for the humans less fortunate than themselves, and by being *humanitarian*—i.e., engaging in action that promotes the welfare of fellow humans.

The Perspective of Society

Moving beyond your local communities, you are also a member of a larger *society*—a group of people organized under the same social system. Societies include subgroups divided into different regions (e.g., north, south, east, west), different population densities (e.g., urban, suburban, rural), and different socioeconomic classes (e.g., level of income, education, and job status). Within a society, there are typically subgroups that are stratified (layered) into different social classes with unequal levels of economic

---

Student Perspective

"I noticed before when I wasn't going to college, they [my family] didn't look at me as highly as a person. But now since I have started college, everybody is lifting me up and saying how proud they [are] of me."

—First-year student, quoted in Franklin, (2002) (61).

"Think globally, act locally."
—Patrick Geddes, Scottish urban planner and social activist

> "It [liberal arts education] shows you how to accommodate yourself to others, how to throw yourself into their state of mind, how to come to an understanding of them. You are at home in any society; you have common ground with every class."
>
> —John Henry Newman, English cardinal and educator

resources. For example, in the United States, the wealthiest 20 percent of the American population controls approximately 50 percent of the total American income, while the 20 percent of Americans with the lowest level of income controls only 4 percent of the nation's wealth (154). Groups occupying lower socioeconomic strata have fewer social and economic resources, and fewer educational and occupational opportunities (57).

REFLECTION 7.4

What do you think is the primary reason poverty exists in human societies? Do you believe that it has the potential to be eliminated? If so, what do you see as the key to its elimination? Or, do you see is it an inevitable element of life in human societies? If so, why?

The Perspective of Culture

Culture can be broadly defined as a distinctive pattern of beliefs and values that are learned by a group of people who share the same social heritage and traditions. In short, culture is the whole way in which a group of people has learned to live; it includes their customary style of speaking (language), fashion, food, art, music, values, and beliefs.

It could be said that the academic divisions of knowledge that comprise the liberal arts curriculum represent different components of human culture that scholars have decided to specialize in and study carefully. Thus, by becoming knowledgeable in these different fields, you become "cultured" or a person "of culture." **Box 7.1** is a summary of key components of culture that a group may share. Notice how these cultural components correspond to the major divisions of knowledge and fields of study in the liberal arts.

Sometimes, the terms "culture" and "society" are used interchangeably as if they were synonymous terms; however, they each refer to a different aspect of humanity. Society is a group of people organized under the same social system. For example, all members of American society are organized under the same system of government, justice, and education. In contrast, culture is what members of a certain group of people actually have in common with respect to their past traditions and current ways of living, regardless of the particular society or social system in which they live (117). For example, cultural differences can exist within the same society, resulting in a "multicultural" society.

A group of people who share the same culture is referred to as an *ethnic group*. Thus, an ethnic group refers to a group of people *who* share the same culture, and culture refers to *what* that ethnic group shares in common. An ethnic group's common cultural characteristics are the result of *socialization*—i.e., they are *learned* and passed on through group members' shared social environment and experiences; they not inherited or transmitted genetically. (Note how the environmental nature of culture is consistent with related terms such as growing living organisms in a "culture" or "cultivating" crops.)

BOX 7.1—KEY COMPONENTS OF CULTURE

- **Linguistic** (Language): How group members communicate through written or spoken word, and through nonverbal communication (body language).

- **Political:** How the group organizes societal authority and uses it to govern itself, make collective decisions, and maintain social order.

- **Economic:** How the material wants and needs of the group are met through the allocation of limited resources, and how wealth is distributed among its members.

- **Geographic:** How the group's physical location influences the nature of their social interactions and affects the way the group adapts to and uses their environment.

- **Aesthetic:** How the group appreciates and expresses artistic beauty and creativity through the fine arts (e.g., visual art, music, theater, literature, and dance).

- **Scientific:** How the group views, understands, and investigates natural phenomena through systematic research (e.g., scientific tests and experiments).

- **Ecological:** How the group views the interrelationship between the biological world (human beings and other living creatures) and the natural world (surrounding physical environment).

- **Anthropological:** How the group's culture originated, evolved, and developed over time.

- **Sociological:** How the group's society is structured or organized into social subgroups and social institutions.

- **Psychological:** How its group members tend to think, feel, and interact; and how their attitudes, opinions, or beliefs have been acquired.

- **Philosophical:** The group's ideas or views on wisdom, goodness, truth, and the meaning or purpose of life.

- **Theological:** The group's conception of, and beliefs about a transcendent, supreme being, and how its members express their shared faith in a supreme being.

The National Perspective

Beyond being a member of society, you are also a citizen of a nation. In a democratic nation, citizens are expected to participate in its governance system—as voters, and in its judicial system—as jurors. It is noteworthy that American citizens between the ages of eighteen and twenty-four have displayed the lowest voter-turnout rate of any age group that is eligible to vote (45). If you are a student in this age group, we strongly encourage you to become an engaged citizen and participate in the voting process. The right to vote is the hallmark of a democratic nation, and having the privilege of being a citizen in a free nation brings with it the responsibility of participating in your country's governance through the voting process. Remember: the original purpose of the liberal arts (and a college education) was to educate citizens broadly and deeply, so they could vote wisely.

The International Perspective

Moving beyond your particular country of citizenship, you are also a member of an international world that includes close to two hundred nations (137). The life of citizens in all nations today is affected by events that cross national borders; boundaries between nations are blurring and breaking down as a result of increased international travel, international trading, and multinational corporations. Furthermore, communication and interaction among citizens of different nations is greater today than at any other time in world history—due in large part to rapid advances in electronic technology (50, 145). The worldwide Web (www) has made today's world a "small world after all" and success in it requires an international perspective.

By learning from and about different nations, you become much more than a citizen of your own country, you become cosmopolitan—a citizen of the world.

The Global Perspective

Broader than an international perspective is the *global* perspective. It includes and unites all members of the human species (almost seven billion and still growing) from all cultures and nation. Despite differences that exist among human groups in terms of their cultural and national experiences, these differences grow from the same soil—they are all rooted in the common ground of our shared humanity.

A global perspective also includes all forms of life inhabiting planet earth and the relationships between these diverse life forms and the earth's natural resources (minerals, air, and water). Humans must remain mindful that they share the earth and its natural resources with approximately 10 million animal species (107) and more than 300,0000 forms of vegetative life (84). As "global citizens" inhabiting the same planet, we have an environmental responsibility to address global issues (e.g., global warming and environmental sustainability), which require striking a healthy balance between making industrial-technological progress, preserving "Mother Earth's" natural resources, and protecting other forms of life that share our planet.

Perspective of the Universe (Cosmos)

Beyond the global perspective is the broadest of all perspectives—the *universe*. Just as we should guard against being ethnocentric—thinking that our culture is the center of humanity, we should also guard against being geocentric—thinking that our planet is the center of the universe. All heavenly bodies do not revolve around planet earth. The sun doesn't rise in the east and set in the west; our planet rotates around the sun to produce our earthly experiences of day and night.

Astronauts who have traveled beyond the earth's force of gravity and viewed the universe from the perspective of outer space often describe their expanded perspective as a "spiritual" experience; and some scholars contend that exploring the universe mentally by reflecting on its massive and mysterious nature, how it may have begun, where it may be going, and whether it will ever end are spiritual questions (165). Whether you view the universe through the physical telescope of astronomy or the spiritual scope of reflective contemplation, it qualifies as the broadest of all social-spatial perspectives developed by the liberal arts.

In sum, the broadening social-spatial perspectives of the liberal arts expand your perception and appreciation of different people and different places. At the same time, they combat the seven types of narrow, close-minded perspectives described in **Box 7.2**.

ELEMENTS OF THE CHRONOLOGICAL PERSPECTIVE: THE PERSPECTIVE OF DIFFERENT TIMES

In addition to expanding your perspective of the word to include other people and places, the liberal arts also stretches your perspective of time to include the past, present, and future.

Historical Perspective

A *historical* perspective is critical for understanding the root causes of the current human condition and world situation. The humanity in the world today is a collective product of social and natural history. Don't forget that our earth is estimated to be more than 4.5 billion years old and our human ancestors date back more than 250,000 years (84). Thus, our current lives represent a very small frame of time in a very long chronological reel. Every human advancement and convenience we enjoy today reflects the collective effort and cumulative knowledge of diverse human groups that has unfolded over thousands of years of history.

By studying the past, we can build on our ancestors' achievements and learn from their mistakes. For example, by understanding the causes and consequences of the holocaust, we can reduce the risk that an atrocious "crime against humanity" of such size and scope will ever happen again.

> "Without exception, the observed changes [during college] involve greater breadth, expansion, and appreciation for the new and different. These changes are eminently consistent with values of a liberal [arts] education, and the evidence for their presence is compelling."
>
> —Ernest Pascarella and Pat Terenzini, *How College Affects Students*

> "Those who cannot remember the past are damned to repeat it."
>
> —George Santayana, Spanish-born American philosopher

> "Yesterday is gone. Tomorrow has not yet come. We have only today. Let us begin."
>
> —Mother Teresa of Calcutta, Albanian Catholic nun and winner of the Nobel Peace Prize

BOX 7.2—SEVEN NARROW VIEWPOINTS COMBATED BY THE BROADENING PERSPECTIVES OF THE LIBERAL ARTS

1. **Egocentrism:** Viewing oneself as the center of all things.
2. **Parochialism** (a.k.a., *provincialism*): Narrow-mindedness and unwillingness to expand one's viewpoints beyond a local perspective.
3. **Regionalism:** Centering on one's own geographical region and favoring everything related to it.
4. **Ethnocentrism:** Belief that one's own cultural customs and values are superior to all others.
5. **Nationalism:** Belief that the interests, needs, or wants of one's own nation should be placed ahead of all other nations.
6. **Anthropocentrism:** Belief that humans are the center of the world and their needs or wants take precedence over all other life forms and planetary resources.
7. **Geocentrism:** Viewing planet Earth as the center of the universe.

Look back at the seven narrow viewpoints combated by the liberal arts. For each perspective, think of a college course you could take that develops this perspective. If you are unsure about what courses are designed to develop any of these perspectives, take a look at the course descriptions in your college catalogue or bulletin (either in print or online).

> "The future is literally in our hands to mold as we like. But we cannot wait until tomorrow. Tomorrow is now."
>
> —Eleanor Roosevelt, United Nations diplomat, humanitarian, and wife of President Franklin D. Roosevelt

Contemporary Perspective

The *contemporary* perspective focuses on understanding the current world situation and the events that comprise today's news. One major goal of a liberal arts education is to increase your understanding the contemporary human condition so that you may have the wisdom to improve it (103). For example, a contemporary perspective will enable you to see that despite historical progress in our nation's acceptance and appreciation of different ethnic and racial groups, the Unites States currently remains a nation deeply divided with respect to differences in culture, religion, and social class (29).

Futuristic Perspective

> "We all inherit the past. We all confront the challenges of the present. We all participate in the making of the future"
>
> —Ernest Boyer and Martin Kaplan, *Educating for Survival: A Call for a Core Curriculum*

The *futuristic* perspective allows you to flash forward and envision what the world will be like years from now. This perspective focuses on such questions as: Will you leave the world a better or worse place for humans who will inhabit after your departure, including our children and grandchildren? How can humans living today move beyond short-term, short-sighted thinking and adopt a long-range vision that anticipates the consequences of their current actions on future generations of humans?

To sum up, a comprehensive chronological perspective brings the past, present, and future into focus on a single screen. It enables us to see how the current world is a short segment of a long temporal sequence that has been shaped by previous events and will shape future events.

> The expanded perspectives on time, place, and people developed by the liberal arts serve to widen, lengthen, and deepen your thinking. You are liberated from thinking in terms of the here and now, and you are empowered to view the world from "long ago and far away."

In light of the information you have read in this chapter, how would you interpret the following statement: "We can't know where we're going until we know where we've been?"

The Synoptic Perspective: Integrating Diverse Perspectives to Form a Unified Whole

The liberal arts not only help you appreciate multiple perspectives; they help you *integrate* them into a meaningful whole (82). Understanding how the perspectives of time, place, and person interrelate to form a unified whole is sometimes referred to as a *synoptic* perspective (43, 70). The word derives from a combination of two different roots: "syn"—meaning "together" (as in the word "synthesize"), and "optic"—meaning "to see." Thus, a *synoptic* perspective literally means to "see things together" or "see the whole." It enables you to see how all the trees come together to form the forest.

By seeing yourself as an integral part of humankind, you become integrated with the whole of humanity; you're able to see how you, as an individual, fit into the "big picture"—the larger scheme of things (69). When we view ourselves as nested within a web of interconnections with other places, people, and times (as shown in **Figures 7.2** and **7.3**), we become aware of the common humanity we all share with all living humans and all humans who have ever lived.

Developing an increased sense of connection with humankind serves to decrease feelings of personal isolation or alienation (18). In his book *The Perfect Education* Kenneth Eble skillfully describes this benefit of a liberal arts education:

It can provide that over-arching life of a people, a community, a world that was going on before the individual came onto the scene and that will continue on after [s]he departs. By such means we come to see the world not alone. Our joys are more intense for being shared. Our sorrows are less destructive for our knowing universal sorrow. Our fears of death fade before the commonness of the occurrence (52).

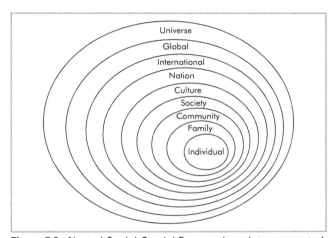

Figure 7.2. Nested Social-Spatial Perspectives: Interconnected People and Places.

Liberating the Development of the "Whole Person"

One of the most frequently cited goals of experiencing the liberal arts is to "know thyself" (44).

In addition to expanding your knowledge of the outer world, they expand knowledge of your inner self. To truly know thyself—to be become fully self-aware—you must know your *whole* self. The liberal arts do this by liberating you from another form of narrowness—a narrow, single-dimensional view of yourself—expanding awareness of the multiplicity of dimensions that comprise the "self." As illustrated in **Figure 7.4**, the human self is comprised of diverse dimensions that join together to form the "whole person."

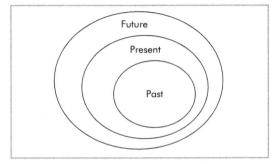

Figure 7.3. Nested Chronological Perspectives: Interconnected Times.

Student Perspective

"I want to see how all the pieces of me come together to make me, physically and mentally."

—College sophomore

Key Dimensions of the Self

• **Intellectual:** Your knowledge, perspectives, and ways of thinking,
• **Emotional:** Your feelings, self-esteem, emotional intelligence, and mental health,
• **Social:** Your interpersonal interactions and relationships,
• **Physical:** Your bodily health and wellness,
• **Vocational:** Your occupational (career) development and satisfaction,
• **Ethical:** Your values, character, and moral convictions,
• **Spiritual:** Your beliefs about the meaning or purpose of life and the hereafter,
• **Personal:** Your identity, self-concept, and capacity for self-management.

Each of the above elements of self plays an influential role in promoting a human being's health, success, and happiness. Research strongly suggests that the quality of an individual's life depends on attention to and development of all key elements of the self. For instance, it has been found that people who are healthy (physically and mentally) and successful (personally and professionally) attend to and integrate different dimensions of their self, enabling them to lead well-rounded and well-balanced lives (41, 66, 70).

One of the primary goals of the liberal arts is to provide a "well-rounded" education that promotes, develops, and integrates the whole person (87). Research on college students confirms that their college experience affects them in multiple ways and develops multiple dimensions of self (25, 58, 126).

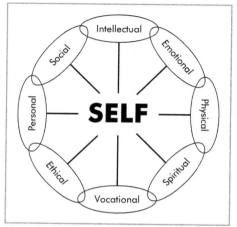

Figure 7.4. Key Elements of Holistic (Whole-Person) Development.

Different elements of self will be discussed separately in this chapter to keep them clear in your mind. However, in reality, they do not operate independently; they are interconnected and influence one another. (This is why the elements of the self in **Figure 7.4** are depicted as links in an interconnected chain.) The self is a diverse, multidimensional entity that has the capacity to develop along a variety of interdependent dimensions (97).

Since wholeness is essential for wellness, success and happiness, take the time to carefully read the following descriptions and specific skills associated with each of the eight elements of holistic development. As you are read the specific skills and qualities listed beneath each of the eight elements, place a checkmark beside any skill that is particularly important to you. You may check more than one skill in each area.

SKILLS AND QUALITIES ASSOCIATED WITH EACH ELEMENT OF HOLISTIC (WHOLE-PERSON) DEVELOPMENT

Intellectual Development: Acquiring knowledge, learning how to learn deeply and to think at a higher level.

Specific Goals and Skills:

- Becoming aware of your intellectual abilities, interests, and learning styles.
- Maintaining attention and concentration.
- Improving your ability to retain knowledge (long-term memory).
- Moving beyond memorization to higher levels of thinking.
- Acquiring effective research skills for accessing information from a variety of sources and systems.
- Viewing issues from multiple angles or viewpoints (psychological, social, political, economic, etc.) in order to attain a balanced, comprehensive perspective.
- Critically evaluating ideas in terms of their truth and value.
- Thinking creatively or imaginatively.
- Responding constructively to differing viewpoints or opposing arguments.
- Detecting and rejecting persuasion tactics that appeal to emotions rather than reason.

Emotional Development: Strengthening your ability to understand, control, and express emotions.

Specific Goals and Skills:

- Dealing with personal emotions in an honest, non-defensive manner.
- Maintaining a healthy balance between emotional control and emotional expression.
- Responding with empathy and sensitivity to emotions experienced by others.
- Dealing effectively with depression.
- Dealing effectively with anger.
- Using effective stress-management strategies to control anxiety and tension.
- Responding effectively to frustrations and setbacks.
- Dealing effectively with fear of failure and poor performance.
- Accepting feedback in a constructive, non-defensive manner.
- Maintaining optimism and enthusiasm.

Social Development: Enhancing the quality and depth of your interpersonal relationships.

Specific Goals and Skills:

- Developing effective conversational skills.
- Becoming an effective listener.

Student Perspective

"Being successful is being balanced in every aspect of your life."

—First-year college student, in response to the question: "What does being successful mean to you?"

"Integration of learning is the ability to connect information from disparate contexts and perspectives—for example, to connect one field of study with another, the past with the present, one part with the whole—and vice versa."

—Wabash National Study of Liberal Arts Education (2007)

Wellness is an integrated method of functioning, which is oriented toward maximizing the potential of the individual.

—H. Joseph Dunn, originator of the term, "wellness," 1959

- Relating effectively to others in one-to-one, small-group, and large-group situations.
- Collaborating effectively with others when working in groups or teams.
- Overcoming shyness.
- Developing more meaningful and intimate relationships.
- Dealing with interpersonal conflicts assertively, rather than aggressively or passively.
- Providing feedback to others in a constructive and considerate manner.
- Relating effectively with others from different cultural backgrounds and lifestyles.
- Developing leadership skills.

Ethical Development: Developing a clear value system for guiding life choices and decisions; building moral character—the ability to make and act on ethical judgments, and to demonstrate consistency between convictions (beliefs) and commitments (actions).

Specific Goals and Skills:

- Gaining deeper self-awareness of your values and ethical assumptions.
- Making personal choices and life decisions based on a meaningful value system.
- Developing the capacity to think and act with personal integrity and authenticity.
- Using electronic technology in an ethical and civil manner.
- Resisting social pressure to act in ways that are inconsistent with your values.
- Treating others in an ethical or morally responsible manner.
- Exercising individual freedom without infringing on the rights of others.
- Developing concern and commitment for human rights and social justice.
- Developing the courage to challenge or confront others who violate human rights and social justice.
- Becoming an ethically responsible citizen.

Physical Development: Applying knowledge about the human body to prevent disease, preserve wellness, and promote peak performance.

Specific Goals and Skills:

- Developing awareness of your physical condition and state of health.
- Applying knowledge about exercise and fitness training to improve your physical and mental health.
- Understanding how sleep patterns affect health and performance.
- Maintaining a healthy balance between work, recreation, and relaxation.
- Acquiring knowledge about nutrition to reduce risk of illness and promote peak performance.
- Gaining knowledge about nutritional imbalances and eating disorders.
- Developing a positive body image.
- Becoming aware of the effects of drugs and their impact on physical and mental well-being.

- Acquiring knowledge about human sexuality, sexual relations, and sexually transmitted diseases.
- Understanding how biological differences affect male-female relationships and gender orientation.

Spiritual Development: Searching for answers to the "big questions," such as the meaning or purpose of life and death, and exploring issues that transcend human life and the physical or material world.

Specific Goals and Skills:

- Developing a philosophy of life or world view about the meaning and purpose of human existence.
- Exploring the unknown or what cannot be completely understood scientifically.
- Exploring the mysteries associated with the origin of the universe.
- Searching for the connection between the self and the larger world or cosmos.
- Searching for the mystical or supernatural—that which transcends the boundaries of the natural world.
- Being open to examining questions relating to death and life after death.
- Being open to examining questions about the possible existence of a supreme being or higher power.
- Acquiring knowledge about different approaches to spirituality and their underlying beliefs or assumptions.
- Understanding the difference and relationship between faith and reason.
- Becoming aware and tolerant of religious beliefs and practices.

Vocational Development: Exploring occupational options, making career choices wisely, and developing skills needed for lifelong career success.

Specific Goals and Skills:

- Understanding the relationship between college majors and careers.
- Using effective strategies for exploring and identifying potential careers.
- Identifying career options that are compatible with your personal values, interests, and talents.
- Acquiring work experience in fields that relate to your career interests.
- Developing an effective resumé and portfolio.
- Adopting effective strategies for identifying personal references and sources for letters of recommendation.
- Acquiring effective job search strategies.
- Using effective strategies for writing letters of inquiry and application to potential employers.
- Developing strategies for performing successfully in personal interviews.
- Acquiring networking skills for connecting with potential employers.

"If you don't stand for something you will fall for anything."

–Malcolm X, African-American Muslim minister, public speaker, and human rights activist

"A man too busy to take care of his health is like a mechanic too busy to take care of his tools."

–Spanish proverb

Student Perspective

"You may think I'm here, living for the 'now' ... but I'm not. Half of my life revolves around the invisible and immaterial. At some point, every one of us has asked the Big Questions surrounding our existence: What is the meaning of life? Is my life inherently purposeful and valuable?"

–College student, quoted in Dalton, et al., 2006 (48)

> "Everyone is a house with four rooms: a physical, a mental, an emotional, and a spiritual. Most of us tend to live in one room most of the time but unless we go into every room every day, even if only to keep it aired, we are not complete."
>
> —Native American proverb

> "Remember, no one can make you feel inferior without your consent."
>
> —Eleanor Roosevelt, human rights activities, author, and diplomat

> "Students may be pushed into careers by their families, while others have picked one just to relieve their anxiety about not having a career choice. Still others may have picked popular or lucrative careers, knowing nothing of what they're really like or what it takes to prepare for them."
>
> —Lee Upcraft, Joni Finney, and Peter Garland, student development specialists

> "I'm a great believer in luck and I find the harder I work, the more I have of it."
>
> —Thomas Jefferson, third president of the United States, and founder of the University of Virginia

Personal Development: Developing positive self-beliefs, attitudes, and habits.

Specific Goals and Skills:

- Developing a strong sense of personal identity and a coherent self-concept. (Who am I?)
- Finding a sense of purpose and direction in life. (Who will I become?)
- Developing self-respect and self-esteem.
- Increasing self-confidence.
- Developing self-efficacy—belief that the outcomes of one's life can be controlled by your own initiative and effort.
- Setting realistic personal goals and priorities.
- Becoming self-motivated and self-disciplined.
- Developing the persistence and perseverance to reach long-range personal goals.
- Acquiring practical skills for managing personal resources (e.g. time and money) effectively and efficiently.
- Becoming independent, self-directed, and self-reliant.

REFLECTION 7.7

Look back and count the number of checkmarks you've placed by each of the eight general areas of self-development. Did you place about the same number of check marks in all eight areas, or were there large discrepancies across the areas?

Based on your number of checkmarks in each area, would you say that your interests in self-development are balanced across different elements of the self, or do they suggest a strong interest in certain dimensions of yourself with much less interest in others?

Do you think you need to, or will eventually begin to, develop a more balanced set of interests across these different dimensions of self-development?

THE CO-CURRICULUM: OUT-OF-CLASS LEARNING EXPERIENCES

The impact of the liberal arts is magnified when you take advantage of the total college environment. This includes not only courses in the curriculum, but also learning experiences outside the classroom—referred to as the *co-curriculum*. Co-curricular experiences include educational discussions you have with your peers and professors outside the classroom, as well as your participation in the variety of events and programs offered on your campus. Research strongly suggests out-of-class learning experiences as being equally important to your overall development as the course curriculum (85, 86); hence, they are referred to as *co*-curricular (not extracurricular) experiences. Studies show that students who become actively involved with the co-curriculum are more likely to:

- Enjoy their college experience;
- Graduate from college; and
- Develop leadership skills that they continue to use beyond college (12).

The learning that takes place in college courses is primarily vicarious—that is, you learn from or through somebody else (e.g., by listening to professors in class and by reading outside of class). While this type of academic learning is valuable, it needs to be complemented and augmented by *experiential* learning—i.e., learning directly through first-hand experiences. For example, leadership cannot be developed solely by listening to lectures and reading books about leadership. In order to fully develop your leadership skills, you need to have leadership *experiences*, such as those developed by "leading a [discussion] group in class, holding office in student government or by being captain of a sports team" (10). College graduates who participated in co-curricular experiences involving leadership while in college consistently report that these experiences allowed them to develop skills that enhanced their job performance and career advancement. College graduates' reports are confirmed by on-the-job evaluations of college alumni, which indicate that co-curricular involvement during college, particularly if it involved leadership experience, is the best predictor of successful managerial performance. Furthermore, students' co-curricular leadership experiences in college are more strongly associated with the managerial success of college graduates than the prestige of the college they attended (126, 127).

PERSONAL EXPERIENCE BY AARON THOMPSON

I consider myself to be a leader and try to lead by example in both my personal and professional life. Although we all have our preferred styles of leadership, a truly effective leader must be able to adapt his or her style to the specific situation and people at hand. The best way to learn how to do this is by acquiring leadership experiences in multiple situations, both inside and outside the classroom. I have found that effective leadership emerges from exposure to a variety of subject areas and ways of learning, including academic ("book learning") and experiential ("hands on" learning). My course work in the liberal arts and my leadership experiences in campus organizations taught me how to understand others, adapt my leadership style to their cultural background, and to appreciate the multiple factors (e.g., personal, social, and global) that are involved in making positive change happen—which is what leadership is all about. The general education you acquire through the liberal arts curriculum and co-curricular experiences will combine to provide you with the broad perspectives and cross-situational skills needed to be an effective leader.

> "The comprehensiveness of general education does not relate simply to knowledge, but to the entire environment in which learning takes place. From the beginning, general education curricula [the liberal arts] have been concerned with the student's total learning environment; the entire community is considered as a resource for general education."
>
> —George Miller (1988), author, *The Meaning of General Education*

Listed in **Box 7.3** below are some of the key programs and services that comprise the co-curriculum accompanied by the primary dimension of the self that they are designed to develop. As you read through the list, note any area(s) in which you think you have leadership potential.

General education includes both the curriculum *and* co-curriculum; it involves strategic use of the *total* college environment, both inside and outside the classroom. Take full advantage of your whole college to develop yourself as a whole person.

"General education reform will go beyond questions of content and formal curriculum, important as they are; its goal will be to create an entire college culture that supports the purposes of general education, within the curriculum and beyond."

–Jerry Gaff, author, *The Second Wave of General Education Reform*

BOX 7.3—CO-CURRICULAR PROGRAMS AND SERVICES PROMOTING DIFFERENT DIMENSIONS OF HOLISTIC DEVELOPMENT

Intellectual Development
Academic advising
Learning centers
Library
Tutoring services
Information technology services
Campus speakers
Concerts, theatre productions, art shows

Social and Emotional Development
Student activities
Student clubs and organizations
Counseling services

Spiritual Development
College chaplain
Campus ministry
Peer ministry

Ethical Development
Judicial review board
Student government
Integrity committees and task forces

Vocational Development
Career development services
Internships programs
Service-learning experiences
Peer counseling
Peer mentoring
Residential life programs
Commuter programs

Physical Development
Student health services
Wellness programs
Campus athletic activities and intramural sports
Work-study programs
Major and career fairs

Personal Development
Financial aid services
Campus workshops on self-management (e.g., managing time or money)

Note: This list represents just a sample of the total number of programs and services that may be available on your campus. As you can see from the list's length, colleges and universities are organized to promote your development in multiple ways. The power of the liberal arts is multiplied when you combine coursework and co-curricular experiences to create a college experience that addresses all key elements of your self.

REFLECTION 7.8

In what area(s) of holistic development mentioned in the above list do you think you have leadership potential? Why?

_____

_____

_____

_____

"To educate liberally, learning experiences must be offered which facilitate maturity of the whole person. These are goals of student development and clearly they are consistent with the mission and goals of liberal education."

–Theodore Berg, author, *Student Development and Liberal Education*

TAKING ACTION: DEVELOPING A GENERAL EDUCATION PLAN FOR MAKING THE MOST OF THE LIBERAL ARTS

Since the liberal arts represent a critical component of your college education, it is a component that should be intentionally planned. Advanced educational planning will put you in a position to maximize the impact of the liberal arts on your personal development and career success.

The first step in this planning process is to become familiar with the general education requirements on your campus. You are likely to find these requirements to be organized into general divisions of knowledge (e.g., humanities, fine arts, natural sciences, behavioral sciences). Within each division, there will be specific courses listed that fulfill the general education requirement(s) for that particular division. In some cases, you will have no choice about the courses you must take to fulfill the division's general education requirements; however, in most cases, you will be free to choose from a group of courses. You can use this freedom to develop a general education plan that intentionally develops all of the "liberating" perspectives of a liberal arts education that have been discussed in this chapter.

If you are uncertain about your college major, use your choices for fulfilling general education requirements to test your interests and abilities in fields that you might consider as a major. For example, your campus may have a general education requirement in social or behavioral sciences that requires you to take two courses in this field, but allows you to choose those two courses from a menu of multiple courses in the field—such as anthropology, economics, political science, psychology, or sociology. If you would consider one of these fields as a possible major, take an introductory course in this subject to test your interest and aptitude for it and, while at the same time, fulfill a general education requirement you needed for graduation. This strategy will allow you to use general education as the main highway to progress toward your final destination (a college degree), while simultaneously allowing you to explore potential majors along the way.

Choose your "free" elective courses strategically to strengthen your liberal arts education. Compared to your previous schooling, the college curriculum will provide you with a broader range of courses to choose from, more freedom of choice, and greater academic decision-making opportunities. Electives are college courses that you elect or choose to take. They come in two forms: restricted electives and free electives. *Restricted* electives are courses that you must take, but they are restricted to a list of possible courses that have been specified by your college as fulfilling a requirement in general education or a requirement in your college major.

Free electives are not required for general education or your college major, but they are needed to enable you to accumulate the total number of college credits for a baccalaureate (bachelor's) degree. Free electives give you complete academic freedom to choose any course in the college catalog. (See **Figure 7.5** for a visual map of how your college education includes courses break out into three key categories: general education courses, major courses, and electives.)

> By connecting the curriculum and co-curriculum, general education launches you on a journey toward two forms of "wholeness": (a) an *inner* wholeness in which different elements of your *self* become connected to form a *whole person*, and (b) an *outer wholeness* that connects your self with the *whole world*. This inner and outer quest for wholeness will lead you to a richer, more fulfilling life that is filled with greater breadth and balance.

> See Exercise 7.1 at the end of this chapter for step-by-step strategies for developing a general education plan that makes the most of the liberal arts.

Enjoy the greater academic freedom you have in college—and employ it to your advantage—use it strategically to make the most of your college experience and college degree.

REFLECTION 7.9

Take a look at **Figure 7.5**, the timeline for completing a bachelor's degree is four years. However, the majority of college students today take five years or longer to complete their degree. What do you think accounts for the fact that most college students do not graduate in four years? Do you think you will graduate in four years? Why?

_____

_____

_____

_____

Your curricular experience is likely to be different than that of any other student because the decisions you make about your elective courses over the course of four academic years is likely to result in a final transcript of courses that is identical to no other graduate. With this freedom of choice comes the responsibility of strategic educational planning and decision-making.

The following suggestions are offered as guidelines for using your free electives in a way that magnifies the power of the liberal arts component of your college education.

"It's good to be rooted in our particular disciplines but not chained to them."

—Carmichael Peters, professor of religious studies and director of the honors program, Chapman University (158)

Take electives that develop *transferable* and durable learning skills, which you can use to promote success throughout your college years and beyond. In addition to taking courses that fulfill general education requirements, you can take elective courses in the liberal arts to further strengthen your repertoire of transferable lifelong skills—such as thinking (e.g., a course in logic or critical thinking), writing (e.g., a course in creative writing), and speaking (e.g., a course in argumentation and debate).

If possible, include *interdisciplinary* courses in your educational plan. Academic disciplines represent a division of labor among scholars in which knowledge is carved up into separate, specialized areas. Deeper and more meaningful learning occurs when bridges are built across these separated and often isolated islands of knowledge. Always be on the lookout to make connections across different courses and be ready to combine the knowledge you acquire from different disciplines to get a more complete understanding of yourself and the world around you.

"The frontiers of knowledge, both in scholarship and the world of work, now call for cross-disciplinary inquiry, analysis, and application. The major issues and problems of our time—from ensuring global sustainability to negotiating international markets to expanding human freedom—transcend individual disciplines."

—AACU (2007)

To help you make cross-disciplinary connections, your college offers some courses that are specifically designed to help you to integrate two or more academic disciplines, which are referred to as *interdisciplinary* courses. For example, psychobiology is an interdisciplinary course that integrates the fields of psychology (focus on the mind) and biology (focus on the body), combining the two in a way that enables you to understand how the mind influences the body and vice versa. Making connections across different subjects not only provides you with a more complete and balanced understanding of the topic. It is also likely that you will find interdisciplinary courses to be a stimulating educational experience.

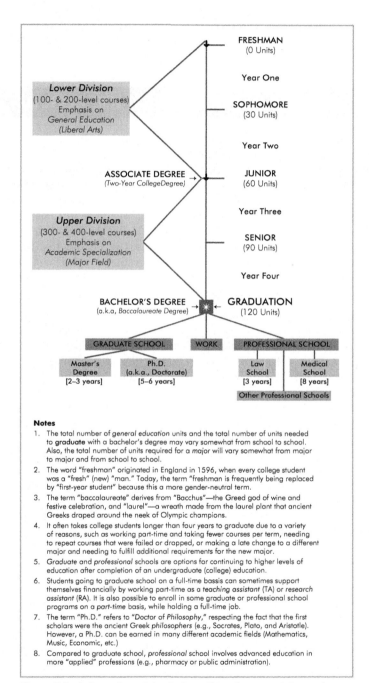

Notes

1. The total number of *general education* units and the total number of units needed to **graduate** with a bachelor's degree may vary somewhat from school to school. Also, the total number of units required for a *major* will vary somewhat from major to major and from school to school.

2. The word "freshman" originated in England in 1596, when every college student was a "fresh" (new) "man." Today, the term "freshman is frequently being replaced by "first-year student" because this a more gender-neutral term.

3. The term "baccalaureate" derives from "Bacchus"—the Greed god of wine and festive celebration, and "laurel"—a wreath made from the laurel plant that ancient Greeks draped around the neek of Olympic champions.

4. It often takes college students longer than four years to graduate due to a variety of reasons, such as working part-time and taking fewer courses per term, needing to repeat courses that were failed or dropped, or making a late change to a different major and needing to fulfill additional requirements for the new major.

5. *Graduate* and *professional* schools are options for continuing to higher levels of education after completion of an undergraduate (college) education.

6. Students going to graduate school on a full-time basis can sometimes support themselves financially by working part-time as a *teaching assistant* (TA) or *research assistant* (RA). It is also possible to enroll in some graduate or professional school programs on a *part-time* basis, while holding a full-time job.

7. The term "Ph.D." refers to "*Doctor of Philosophy*," respecting the fact that the first scholars were the ancient Greek *philosophers* (e.g., Socrates, Plato, and Aristotle). However, a Ph.D. can be earned in many different academic fields (Mathematics, Music, Economic, etc.)

8. Compared to graduate school, *professional* school involves advanced education in more "applied" professions (e.g., pharmacy or public administration).

Figure 7.5. A Snapshot of the College Experience and Beyond.

Research indicates that students who participate in interdisciplinary courses report greater gains in learning and greater satisfaction with the learning experience (12, 148).

PERSONAL EXPERIENCE BY JOE CUSEO

After my first five years of being a college professor in psychology, I came to realize that the most important issues in the world and the issues that mattered most to students were those that extended beyond the boundaries of a single academic field or discipline. Almost every time I mentioned something in one of my psychology courses that happened to relate to an idea that my students were discussing in another course, they would perk up and excitedly point out (or blurt out): "We were just talking about this in _____ (some other) class!" I wasn't sure if I should feel thrilled or depressed when students reported these connections. On the one hand, I was happy that they were seeing the connection and were excited about it; however, on the other hand, the amount of sheer surprise and exhilaration they displayed whenever they saw a connection suggested to me that these connections were a very rare occurrence!

As a result of these observations, I tried to make a more conscious attempt to connect material in my psychology courses with ideas covered in other subject areas. I found that making these connections further increased student interest in the topics I covered in my psychology courses. I became so interested in the idea of making connections between my field and other fields of study that I took a new teaching position at a college which emphasized interdisciplinary, team-taught courses. I went on to team-teach interdisciplinary courses such as: Humor and the Comic Spirit (combining psychology, literature, and film), Sports in American Society (psychology, sociology, and philosophy), Drug Use and Abuse (psychology and criminal justice), and Mind, Brain, and Behavior (psychology and biology). These courses proved to be among my most effective and enjoyable teaching experiences. The students were excited about taking them and making connections across different fields, and the instructors learned a lot from each other. If you have the opportunity to take an interdisciplinary course or participate in an interdisciplinary program, take advantage of it; you should find it to be both a unique and stimulating learning experience.

Your campus may also offer interdisciplinary senior seminars or "capstone courses" designed to integrate general education with your specialized major (47). If such a course is available on your campus, strongly consider taking it. Such senior-level interdisciplinary courses can "tie it altogether" and cultivate the synoptic perspective described in this chapter (**p. 130**), enabling you to see how different disciplinary perspectives come together to form the "big picture."

Enroll in *service-learning* courses designed to connect learning in the classroom with volunteer service in the community. For example, a sociology course may include assignments involving volunteer service in the local community that you reflect on, and relate to course material through writing assignments or class discussions. Research indicates that students who participate in service-learning courses experience strong gains in multiple areas of self-development, including critical thinking and leadership (13, 147).

Consider pursuing a college *minor* in a liberal arts field that will complement and broaden your major. Most colleges allow you the option of completing a minor along with your major. A college minor usually requires about one-half the number of credits (units) that are required for a college major. Taking a cluster of courses in a field outside your major can be an effective way to strengthen your resume and promote your employment prospects; it demonstrates your versatility and allows you to acquire knowledge and skills that may be underemphasized in your major. For instance, students majoring in such fields as business or computer science may take a cluster of courses in fine arts or humanities to develop skills and perspectives that are not strongly emphasized in their own major field (e.g., a foreign language or international studies course to enhance their career prospects in today's global economy).

If you have interest and talent in a liberal arts field, consider pursuing it as a college *major*. A commonly held myth is that all you can do with a major in a liberal arts field is to teach that subject (e.g., English majors become English teachers; history majors become history teachers). However, the truth is that students majoring in liberal arts fields enter, advance, and prosper in a wide variety of careers. Among students with liberal arts majors are such notable college graduates as:

> "The first week of law school, one of my professors stressed the importance of 'researching, analyzing and writing.' I thought this was an interesting thing to say, because English majors learn and practice these skills in every class."
>
> —English major attending law school (158)

- Jill Barad (English major), CEO, Mattel Toys

- Steve Case (political science major), CEO, America Online

- Brian Lamb (speech major), CEO, C-Span

- Willie Brown (liberal studies major), Mayor, San Francisco (74).

Significant numbers of liberal arts majors are employed in positions that involve marketing, human resources, or public affairs (23, 157). Research also reveals that the career mobility and career advancement of liberal arts majors working in the corporate world are comparable to business majors. For example, liberal arts majors are just as likely to advance to the highest levels of corporate leadership as majors in pre-professional fields such as business and engineering (127).

Students majoring in a liberal arts field can further increase their marketability by combining their major with a minor or cluster of courses in a more "applied" pre-professional field. For example, students majoring in the fine arts (music, theatre) or humanities (English, history) may take courses in the fields of mathematics (e.g., statistics), technology (e.g., computer science), and business (e.g., economics) to acquire knowledge and skills that are not typically emphasized by their major. (Some campuses offer business courses that are reserved specifically for liberal arts majors.) Employment and career opportunities for non-business majors are enhanced if they have some course work in business (e.g., economics, business administration) (149). Liberal arts majors can further increase their employment prospects by completing an internship. Research shows that students in all majors who have an internship while in college are more likely to develop career-relevant work skills and find immediate employment after graduation (127).

> The liberal arts broaden, rather than narrow, your future career possibilities. If you have a passion for and talent in a liberal arts field, do not be dismayed or discouraged by those who may question your choice by asking: "What are you going to do with a degree in *that* major?"

Furthermore, liberal arts majors are not restricted to pursuing a degree in graduate school or professional school that is in the same field as their college major. For example, English majors can still go to graduate school in an academic field other than English, or go to law school, or get a master's degree in business administration. In fact, it is common to find that the majority of graduate students in master's of business administration (MBA) programs were not business majors (51).

JOURNAL ENTRIES

Journal Entry 7.1

How would you interpret the meaning or message of the following quotes?

"It is such good fortune for people in power that people do not think."
—Adolf Hitler, German dictator

"Those who cannot remember the past are damned to repeat it."
—George Santayana, Spanish-born American philosopher

"A liberal [arts] education frees a person from the prison-house of class, race, time, place, background, family, and nation."
—Robert Hutchins, former dean of Yale Law School and president of the University of Chicago

Journal Entry 7.2

I am going to college to . . .
I decided to attend this particular college or university because . . .

Journal Entry 7.3

What would you say in response to a classmate who asks you the following question: "Aren't you glad to get all your general education (liberal arts) courses out of the way and over with, so you can finally get into courses that actually relate to your major and future career?"

Journal Entry 7.4

Reflect on your responses to the reflection questions in this chapter. Which one(s) do you find to be most personally significant or revealing? Why?

EXERCISE 1. DEVELOPING A GENERAL EDUCATION PLAN FOR MAKING THE MOST OF THE LIBERAL ARTS

Highlight the specific courses in the catalog that you plan to take to fulfill your general education requirements in each area of the liberal arts. Before making a course selection, carefully read the description of the course in your college catalog or bulletin.

Select general education courses that will enable you to attain all of the *broadening perspectives* **developed by a liberal arts education.** For example, strategically select courses that provide you with a *societal* perspective (e.g., sociology), a *national* perspective (e.g., political science), an *international* perspective (e.g., cultural geography), and a *global* perspective (e.g., ecology). (All of the broadening perspectives developed by the liberal arts are described on page 129.)

Use the form below as a checklist to ensure that all key perspectives are included and that there are no "blind spots" in your general education plan.

Broadening Social-Spatial Perspectives (See pp. 125–129 for further descriptions of these perspectives.)	Course Developing This Perspective (Read the course descriptions in your Catalog to identify a general education requirement that develops each of these perspectives.)
Self	
Family	
Community	
Society	
Culture	
Nation	
International	
Global	
Universe (Cosmos)	
Broadening Chronological Perspectives (See pp. 129–132 for detailed description of these perspectives.)	**Course Developing This Perspective** (Read the course descriptions in your Catalog to identify a general education requirement that develops each of these perspectives.)
Historical	
Contemporary	
Futuristic	

Select general education courses that will enable you to develop yourself as a *whole person.* Enroll in courses that cover all the key dimensions of self-development and allow you to develop as a whole person. For instance, include courses that promote your *emotional* development (e.g., stress management), *social* development (e.g., interpersonal relationships), *mental* development (e.g., critical thinking), *physical* development (e.g., nutrition, self-defense), and *spiritual* development (e.g., world religions; death and dying).

Remember that development of the "whole self" also includes co-curricular learning experiences outside the classroom (e.g., leadership and volunteer experiences). Be sure to include these experiences as part of your holistic-development plan. Your student handbook probably represents the best resource for information about co-curricular experiences offered by your college.

Use the form below as a checklist below for ensuring that your educational plan includes all key elements of holistic ("whole person") development.

Dimensions of Self (See p. 132 for description of these dimensions.)	Course or Co-curricular Experience Developing this Dimension of Self (Consult your student handbook for co-curricular experiences.)
Intellectual (Cognitive)	
Emotional	
Social	
Ethical	
Physical	
Spiritual	
Vocational	
Personal	

Chapter 8

Critical Thinking

Developing Critical Skills for the Twenty-First Century

What are we to believe? What should we accept with reservations, and what should we dismiss outright? As we gather information about the world via the media (e.g., television, radio, the Internet, and newspapers and magazines), we tend to take much of the information at face value, ignoring the fact that the information has been selected and organized (shaped and edited) by the person or organization presenting it. People are often lulled into a false sense of security, believing that the sources of information they are basing their decisions on are objective and truthful (Chaffee, 1998). Discovering the answers to the six important questions that reporters are trained to answer near the beginning of every news article—who, what, where, when, why, and how—is not enough to allow us to think critically about complex and sometimes controversial topics. To engage in thinking at this higher level, one needs to know how to ask questions and think independently.

The authors of this chapter view critical thinking developmentally as a set of complex thinking skills that can be improved through knowledge and guided practice. Thinking skills are categorized in the problem-solving/decision-making set of life-skills necessary for information seeking. These skills include information assessment and analysis; problem identification, solution, implementation, and evaluation; goal setting; systematic planning and forecasting; and conflict resolution. Presented in this chapter are developmental thinking models, critical thinking and problem-solving models, and information about the construction and evaluation of an argument.

THINKING AS A DEVELOPMENTAL PROCESS

Cognitive psychologists study the development and organization of knowledge and the role it plays in various mental activities (e.g., reading, writing, decision making, and problem solving). What is knowledge? Where it is stored? How do you construct mental representations of your world? The personal answers to these and other questions are often found for the first time in college when students focus their attention on what they know and how they know it.

Models of Knowledge

Different forms of knowledge interact when you reason and construct a mental representation of the situation before you. Joanne Kurfiss (1988) wrote about the following three kinds of knowledge.

- **Declarative knowledge** is knowing facts and concepts. Kurfiss recognizes the considerable amount of declarative knowledge that students acquire through their college courses. To move students to a higher level of thinking, instructors generally ask students to write analytical essays, instead of mere summaries, to explain the knowledge they have acquired in the course.

- **Procedural knowledge, or strategic knowledge,** is knowing how to use declarative knowledge to do something (e.g., interpret textbooks, study, navigate the Internet, and find a major).

- **Metacognition** is knowing what knowledge to use to control one's situation (e.g., how to make plans, ask questions, analyze the effectiveness of learning strategies, initiate change). If students' metacognitive skills are not well developed, students may not be able to use the full potential of their knowledge when studying in college.

William Perry

You may have read about the developmental theorist William Perry. In his research on college-age students, Perry distinguished a series of stages that students pass through as they move from simple to complex levels of thinking. Basically, they move from *dualism*, the simplest stage, where knowledge is viewed as a factual quality dispensed by authorities (professors), to *multiplicity*, in which the student recognizes the complexity of knowledge (e.g., he or she understands that there is more than one perspective of the bombing of Hiroshima or the role of the United States in the Vietnam war) and believes knowledge to be subjective, to *relativism*, where the student reaches an understanding that some views make greater sense than other views. Relativism is reflected in situations where a student has made a commitment to the particular view they have constructed of the world, also known as *Weltanschauung*. Constructing a personal *critical epistemology* is an essential developmental task for undergraduates, according to Perry (Chaffee, 1998).

Bloom's Taxonomy of Thinking and Learning

Benjamin Bloom (1956) and his associates at the University of Chicago developed a classification system, or taxonomy, to explain how we think and learn (see Figure 8.1). The taxonomy consists of six levels of thinking arranged in a hierarchy, beginning with simple cognitive tasks (knowledge) and moving up to more complex thinking (evaluation). Thinking at each level is dependent on thinking skills at lower levels.

One of the reasons that college students often experience difficulty learning and studying during their first semester is that the learning and study strategies from high school are not necessarily effective in the new setting. In high school you are generally asked to memorize, comprehend, and interpret information. In college you are asked to do all that and more. To be successful in a college setting, you need to learn how to apply, analyze, synthesize, and evaluate information. Let's look at Bloom's six levels of learning and thinking.

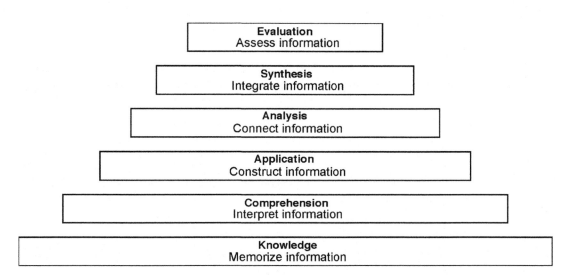

Figure 8.1 Bloom's Hierarchy of Thinking

Knowledge Level. If you are cramming for a test, chances are good that you are thinking at the knowledge level, the lowest level of thinking. You are basically attempting to memorize a lot of information in a short amount of time. If you are asked on the test to identify, name, select, define, or list particular bits of information, you might do okay, but you will most likely forget most of the information soon after taking the test.

Comprehension Level. When you are classifying, describing, discussing, explaining, and recognizing information, you are in the process of interpreting information. At the bottom of your lecture notes for the day, see if you can summarize your notes using your own words. In doing so, you can develop a deeper understanding of the material just covered in class.

Application Level. At this third level of thinking, you are constructing knowledge by taking previously learned information and applying it in a new and different way to solve problems. Whenever you use a formula or a theory to solve a problem, you are thinking at the application level. Some words used to describe how you process information at this level are *illustrate, demonstrate,* and *apply.* To increase thinking at the application level, develop the habit of thinking of examples to illustrate concepts presented in class or during reading. Be sure to include the examples in your notations in your books and notes.

Analysis Level. When you analyze information, you break the information down into parts and then look at the relationships among the parts. In your literature class, if you read two plays from different time periods and then compare and contrast them in terms of style and form, you are analyzing. When you analyze, you connect pieces of information. You *discriminate, correlate, classify,* and *infer.*

Synthesis Level. When you are synthesizing information, you are bringing together all the bits of information that you have analyzed to create a new pattern or whole. When you synthesize, you *hypothesize, predict, generate,* and *integrate.* Innovative ideas often emerge at the synthesis level of thinking.

Evaluation Level. This is the highest level of thinking according to Bloom's taxonomy. When you evaluate, you judge the validity of the information. You may be evaluating opinions ("Is that person really an expert?") or biases.

Answer the following questions to test your understanding of Bloom's taxonomy. According to Bloom's taxonomy of thinking, which level of thinking would you be engaging in if you were asked to

- Read an article about an upcoming candidate in a local election and then summarize the candidate's characteristics?
- View a video about hate and prejudice and then write an essay about how you can confront hate and prejudice on a personal level?
- Determine the most effective way for you to study?
- Identify and define the parts of the forebrain?
- Judge a new campus parking policy created by your college's parking services?

MODELS OF CRITICAL THINKING/ PROBLEM SOLVING

Critical Thinking

One of the primary objectives of a college education is to develop the skills necessary to become an autonomous, independent learner. Critical thinking prepares you to be an independent thinker. To ensure that you are thinking critically, you can follow the CRITICAL model developed by the authors (Glauser & Ginter, 1995). This model identifies important steps and key ideas in critical thinking: construction, refocus, identify, think through, insight, conclusions, accuracy, and lens.

Construction. Each of us constructs a unique view of the world. Our construction, or perception, of the world is based on our thoughts and beliefs. Our cultural background influences our perceptions, and they form the basis of our assumptions. For example, you might assume that a college education can help you to get a better job. How do you know this? Maybe you know this because a parent or teacher told you so. If this is the only bit of information on which you are basing your assumption about the value of a college education, you have not engaged in critical thinking. If you had engaged in critical thinking, you would have analyzed and synthesized information that you gathered about the benefits of a college education. If you have based your decision to attend this college on good critical thinking, then you will know why you are here and will more likely be motivated to graduate.

Perceptions of information, behaviors, and situations are often based on unexamined assumptions that are inaccurate and sketchy. The first step in this model is to investigate personal underlying biases that are inherent in your assumptions about any issue before you. For example, let us say that you are with some friends and the topic of surrogate motherhood comes up. Maybe you have already formed an opinion about the issue. This opinion could be based on strong critical thinking, but if not, then your opinion is merely a strong, personal feeling. If you choose to look at surrogate motherhood from a critical-thinking perspective, you would begin by examining your own thoughts and beliefs about motherhood and surrogacy. No matter what issue is before you (e.g., racism, abortion, euthanasia, genetic engineering), the process is the same; begin by examining your own assumptions. As you do this, look for biases and other patterns of thinking that have become cemented over time and are influencing the way you view the issue.

Refocus. Once you have acknowledged some of your own biases, refocus your attention so you can hear alternative viewpoints. Refocus by reading additional information, talking to people with opposing viewpoints, or maybe watching a movie or a video. You are trying to see other people's perspectives. Read carefully, and listen carefully with the intent to learn. Can you think of any books that you have read or movies that have influenced the way you see a particular issue?

To illustrate the effect of refocusing, list three sources of additional information (e.g., book, movie, another person, newspaper, or experience) that changed your mind about something important to you. Explain how it changed you.

1. _____

   _____

   _____

2. _____

   _____

   _____

3. _____

   _____

   _____

Identify. Identifying core issues and information is the third step of critical thinking. After you have gathered all your additional information representing different viewpoints, think over the information carefully. Are there any themes that emerge? What does the terminology related to the issue tell you? Look at all the facts and details. We all try to make sense out of what we hear and see by arranging information into a pattern, a story that seems reasonable. There is a tendency to arrange the information to fit our perceptions and beliefs. When we engage in critical thinking, we are trying to make sense of all the pieces, not just the ones that happen to fit our own preconceived pattern.

Think Through. The fourth step of critical thinking requires that you think through all the information gathered. The task is to distinguish between what is fact and what is fiction and what is relevant and not relevant. Examine premises and decide if they are logically valid. Look for misinformation. Maybe you have gathered inaccurate facts and figures. Check the sources for reliability. Asking questions is a large part of good critical thinking.

This step of the model is where you analyze and synthesize information. You are continually focusing your attention in and out, similar to the way you might focus a camera. This step of the critical-thinking process can be very creative. You are using both parts of the brain. The right brain is being speculative, suspending judgment, and challenging definitions. The left brain is analyzing the information received in a more traditional style, thinking logically and sequentially. While thinking critically, have you detected any over-generalizations (e.g., women are more emotional and less rational than men are) or over-simplifications (e.g., the high dropout rate at the local high school is due to an increase in single-parent families)?

Insight. Once key issues have been identified and analyzed, it is time to develop some insight into some of the various perspectives on the issue. Sometimes some of the best insights come when you can sit back and detach yourself from all the information you have just processed. Often new meanings will emerge that provide a new awareness. You might find that you have developed some empathy for others that may not have been there before. When you hear the term "broken home," what images do you conjure up? How do you think a child who resides with a single parent or alternates between divorced parents' homes feels when hearing that term applied to his or her situation? A lot of assumptions are embedded in such concepts.

Conclusions. If you do not have sufficient evidence to support a decision, suspend judgment until you do. An important tenet of critical thinking is not to jump to conclusions. If you do, you may find that you have a fallacy in your reasoning. A fallacy is an instance of incorrect reasoning. Maybe you did not have sufficient evidence to support your decision to major in biology, or maybe your conclusions about the issue of euthanasia do not follow logically from your premise. Also look at the conclusions you have drawn, and ask yourself if they have any implications that you might need to rethink? Do you need to consider alternative interpretations of the evidence?

Accuracy. You are not through thinking! In addition to looking for fallacies in your reasoning, you also need to consider some other things.

- Know the difference between reasoning and rationalizing. Which thinking processes are your conclusions based on?
- Know the difference between what is true and what seems true based on the emotional attachment you have to your ideas and beliefs.
- Know the difference between opinion and fact. Facts can be proven; opinions cannot.

Lens. In this last step of critical thinking, you have reached the understanding that most issues can be viewed from multiple perspectives. These perspectives form a lens that offers a more encompassing view of the world around you. Remember that there are usually many solutions to a single issue.

Problem Solving

Problem solving involves critical thinking. Are problem solving and critical thinking the same? Not really. Problem solving is about having the ability and skills to apply knowledge to pragmatic problems encountered in all areas of your life. If you were trying to solve a financial problem or decide whether or not to change roommates, you probably would not need a model of thinking as extensive as the one previously described. The following steps offer an organized approach to solving less complex problems.

1. Identify the problem. Be specific and write it down.
2. Analyze the problem.
3. Identify alternative ways to solve the problem.
4. Examine alternatives.
5. Implement a solution.
6. Evaluate.

Identify the problem. What exactly is the problem you wish to solve? Is it that your roommate is driving you crazy, or is it that you want to move into an apartment with your friend next semester? Be specific.

Analyze the problem. Remember, analysis means looking at all the parts. It is the process by which we select and interpret information. Be careful not to be too selective or simplistic in your thinking. Look at all the facts and details. For example, suppose you want to move into an apartment with your friends. Do you need permission from anyone to do so? Can you afford to do this? Can you get a release from your dorm lease? Your answer to all the questions might be yes, with the exception of being able to afford it. You want to move, so now the problem is a financial one. You need to come up with the financial resources to follow through on your decision.

Identify alternative ways to solve the problem. Use convergent and divergent thinking. You are engaging in **convergent thinking** when you are narrowing choices to come up with the correct solution (e.g., picking the best idea out of three). You are engaging in **divergent thinking** when you are thinking in terms of multiple solutions. Mihaly Csikszentmihalyi (1996) says, "Divergent thinking leads to no agreed-upon solution. It involves fluency, or the ability to generate a great quantity of ideas; flexibility, or the ability to switch from one perspective to another; and originality in picking unusual associations of ideas" (1996, p. 60). He concludes that a person whose thinking has these qualities is likely to come up with more innovative ideas.

Brainstorming is a great way to generate alternative ways to solve problems. This creative problem-solving technique requires that you use both divergent and convergent thinking. Here are some steps to use if you decide to brainstorm.

• Describe the problem.
• Decide on the amount of time you want to spend brainstorming (e.g., 10 minutes).
• Relax (remember some of the best insights come in a relaxed state).

- Write down everything that comes to your mind (divergent thinking).
- Select your best ideas (convergent thinking).
- Try one out! (If it does not work, try one of the other ideas you selected.)

Students have successfully used the process of brainstorming to decide on a major, choose activities for spring break, develop topics for papers, and come up with ideas for part-time jobs. Being creative means coming up with atypical solutions to complex problems.

Examine alternatives. Make judgments about the alternatives based on previous knowledge and the additional information you now have.

Implement a solution. Choose one solution to your problem and eliminate the others for now. (If this one fails, you may want to try another solution later.)

Evaluate. If the plan is not as effective as you had hoped, modify your plan or start the process over again. Also look at the criteria you used to judge your alternative solutions.

Think of a problem that you are currently dealing with. Complete Exercise 1 ("Creating Breakthroughs") at the end of the chapter. This is an opportunity to try to solve a problem using this six-step problem-solving model.

ARGUMENTS

Critical thinking involves the construction and evaluation of arguments. An argument is a form of thinking in which reasons (statements and facts) are given in support of a conclusion. The reasons of the argument are known as the **premises**. A good argument is one in which the premises are logical and support the conclusion. The validity of the argument is based on the relationship between the premises and the conclusion. If the premises are not credible or do not support the conclusion, or the conclusion does not follow from the premises, the argument is considered to be **invalid** or fallacious. Unsound arguments (based on fallacies) are often persuasive because they can appeal to our emotions and confirm what we want to believe to be true. Just look at commercials on television. Alcohol advertisements show that you can be rebellious, independent, and have lots of friends, fun, and excitement by drinking large quantities of alcohol—all without any negative consequences. Intelligence is reflected in the capacity to acquire and apply knowledge. Even sophisticated, intelligent people are influenced by fallacious advertising.

Invalid Arguments

It is human irrationality, not a lack of knowledge, that threatens human potential.
—Raymond Nickerson, in J. K. Kurfiss, *Critical Thinking*

In the book *How to Think About Weird Things,* Theodore Schick and Lewis Vaughn (1999) suggest that you can avoid holding irrational beliefs by understanding the ways in which an argument can fail. First, an argument is fallacious if it contains **unacceptable premises,** premises that are as incredible as the claim they are supposed to support. Second, if they contain **irrelevant premises,** or premises that are not logically related to the conclusion, they are also fallacious. Third, they are fallacious if they contain **insufficient premises,** meaning that the premises do not eliminate reasonable grounds for doubt. Schick and Vaughn recommend that whenever someone presents an argument, you check to see if the premises are acceptable, relevant, and sufficient. If not, then the argument presented is not logically compelling, or valid.

Schick and Vaughn abstracted from the work of Ludwig F. Schlecht the following examples of fallacies based on illogical premises.

Unacceptable Premises

- **False dilemma** (also known as the either/or fallacy) presumes that there are only two alternatives from which to choose when in actuality there are more than two. For example: You are either with America or against us. You are not with America, therefore you are against us.

- **Begging the question** is also referred to as arguing in a circle. A conclusion is used as one of the premises. For example: "You should major in business, because my advisor says that if you do, you will be guaranteed a job." "How do you know this?" "My advisor told me that all business majors find jobs."

Irrelevant Premises

- **Equivocation** occurs when the conclusion does not follow from the premises due to using the same word to mean two different things. For example: Senator Dobbs has always been *patriotic* and shown a deep affection and respect for his country. Now, though, he is criticizing the government's foreign policy. This lack of *patriotism* makes him unworthy of reelection.

- **Appeal to the person** (*ad hominem,* or "to the man") occurs when a person offers a rebuttal to an argument by criticizing or denigrating its presenter rather than constructing a rebuttal based on the argument presented. As Schick and Vaughn note, "Crazy people can come up with perfectly sound arguments, and sane people can talk nonsense" (1999, p. 287).

- **Appeal to authority** is when we support our views by citing experts. If the person is truly an expert in the field for which they are being cited, then the testimony is probably valid. How often do you see celebrities endorsing products? Is an argument valid just because someone cites an article from the *New York Times* or the *Wall Street Journal* for support?

- **Appeal to the masses** is a type of fallacy that occurs when support for the premise is offered in the form, "It must be right because everybody else does it." For example: It's okay to cheat. Every college student cheats sometime during their undergraduate years.

- **Appeal to tradition** is used as an unsound premise when we argue that something is true based on an established tradition. For example: It's okay to drink large quantities of alcohol and go wild during Spring Break. It's what students have always done.

- **Appeal to ignorance** relies on claims that if no proof is offered that something is true, then it must be false, or conversely, that if no proof is offered that something is false, then it must be true. Many arguments associated with religions of the world are based on irrelevant premises that appeal to ignorance.

- **Appeal to fear** is based on a threat, or "swinging the big stick." For example: If you don't start studying now, you will never make it through college. Schick and Vaughn remind us, "Threats extort; they do not help us arrive at the truth" (1999, p. 289).

Insufficient Premises

- **Hasty generalizations** are often seen when people stereotype others. Have you noticed that most stereotypes are negative? When we describe an individual as pushy, cheap, aggressive, privileged, snobbish, or clannish and then generalize that attribute to the group we believe that person belongs to, we are committing a hasty generalization.
- **Faulty analogy** is the type of fallacy committed when there is a claim that things that have similar qualities in some respects will have similarities in other respects. For example: Dr. Smith and Dr. Wilson may both teach at the same college, but their individual philosophies about teaching and learning may be very different.
- **False cause** fallacies occur when a causal relationship is assumed despite a lack of evidence to support the relationship. Do you have a special shirt or hat that you wear on game days to influence the odds that the team you are cheering for wins?

CLOSING REMARKS

Belgian physicist Ilya Prigogine was awarded the Nobel Prize for his theory of dissipative structures. Part of the theory "contends that friction is a fundamental property of nature and nothing grows without it—not mountains, not pearls, not people. It is precisely the quality of fragility, he says, the capacity for being shaken up, that is paradoxically the key to growth. Any structure—whether at the molecular, chemical, physical, social, or psychological level that is insulated from disturbance is also protected from change. It becomes stagnant. Any vision—or any thing—that is true to life, to the imperatives of creation and evolution, will not be 'unshakable'" (Levoy, 1997 p. 8).

Throughout this textbook you will read about how change affects you now as a student in college and throughout the rest of your life. Education is about learning how to look and how to listen to what instructors, books, television, and other sources of information are saying, and to discover whether or not what they are saying is true or false.

In reference to education and learning, the philosopher Jiddu Krishnamurti said that there should be "an intent to bring about change in the mind which means you have to be extraordinarily critical. You have to learn never to accept anything which you yourself do not see clearly" (1974, p. 18). He said that education is always more than learning from books, or memorizing some facts, or the instructor transmitting information to the student. Education is about critical thinking, and critical thinking is the foundation of all learning.

Critical thinking is thinking that moves you beyond simple observations and passive reporting of those observations. It is an active, conscious, cognitive process in which there is always intent to learn. It is the process by which we analyze and evaluate information, and it is how we make good sense out of all the information that we are continually bombarded with.

Marcia Magolda believes that critical thinking fosters qualities such as maturity, responsibility, and citizenship. "Both the evolving nature of society and the student body has led to reconceptualizations of learning outcomes and processes. In a postmodern society, higher education must prepare students to shoulder their moral and ethical responsibility to confront and wrestle with the complex problems they will encounter in today and tomorrow's world. Critical, reflective thinking skills, the ability to gather and evaluate evidence, and the ability to make one's own informed judgments are essential learning outcomes if students are to get beyond relativity to make informed judgments in a world in which multiple perspectives are increasingly interdependent and 'right action' is uncertain and often in dispute." (Magolda & Terenzini, 1999, p. 3)

SOURCES

Bloom, B. (1956). *Taxonomy of educational objectives: The classification of educational goals. Handbook I: Cognitive domain.* London: Longmans.

Chaffee, J. (1998). *The thinker's way.* Boston: Little, Brown.

Csikszentmihalyi, M. (1996). *Creativity.* New York: HarperCollins.

DiSpezio, M. (1998). *Challenging critical thinking puzzles.* New York: Sterling.

Glauser, A., & Ginter, E. J. (1995, October). *Beyond hate and intolerance.* Paper presented at the southeastern Conference of Counseling Center Personnel, Jekyll Island, GA.

Johnson, D., & Johnson, F. (2000). *Joining together.* Boston: Allyn and Bacon.

Krishnamurti, J. (1974). *Krishnamurti on education.* New York: Harper & Row.

Kurfiss, J. G. (1988). *Critical thinking: Theory, research, practice, and possibilities. Critical thinking,* 2. Washington, DC: ASHE-Eric Higher Education Reports.

Levoy, Gregg. (1997). *Callings.* New York: Three Rivers Press.

Magolda, M. B., & Terenzini, P. (1999). Learning and teaching in the twenty-first century: Trends and implications for practice. In C. S. Johnson & H. E. Cheatham (Eds.), *Higher education trends for the next century: A research agenda for student's success.* Retrieved November 30, 1999, from http://www.acpa.nche.edu/ seniorscholars/trends/trends.htn

Perry, W. (1970). *Forms of intellectual and ethical development during the college years: A scheme.* New York: Holt, Rinehart and Winston.

Schick, T., & Vaughn, L. (1999). *How to Think About Weird Things: Critical Thinking for a New Age.* Mountain View, CA: Mayfield.

NAME: _____ **DATE:** _____

EXERCISE 1. CREATING BREAKTHROUGHS

Select a problem related to being a student at your college.

1. State the problem.

2. Analyze the problem.

3. Brainstorm alternative solutions.

4. Examine your alternatives. Pick the five best options from your brainstorming and record them below.

a. _____

b. _____

c. _____

d. _____

e. _____

When you consider your problem and the list of options that you have created, what kind of criteria do you want to use in judging your options? For example, let us say that you stated your problem as needing money to stay in school. The best five options you came up with for getting money to stay in school were to work full time and go to evening school, alternate between going to school for a year and then working for a year, take out a student loan, study hard and raise your GPA to obtain a scholarship, and beg your family for money. The criteria you choose to judge your options might be that you do not want to be really stressed out, you want your plan to be reliable, and you want to owe as little as possible upon graduation.

List three criteria you will use to evaluate your options.

C1. _____

C2. _____

C3. _____

Now, using a scale from 1–5, rate each option using your criteria, with 5 being the highest rating.

OPTIONS	C1	C2	C3	TOTAL (C1 + C2 + C3)
a.				
b.				
c.				
d.				
e.				

EXERCISE 1 (continued)

What are your two best options?

_____

_____

5. Implement a solution. Which option will you choose to act on?

_____

What kinds of resources will you need? (List four.)

_____

_____

_____

_____

List some of your planning steps.

_____

_____

_____

_____

_____

_____

_____

_____

_____

_____

6. Evaluate. Look over what you have listed as resources and planning steps, and decide if you forgot something important. Indicate below if you believe the plan you have come up with is feasible, and whether you left something out that now should become part of your solution.

EXERCISE 2. CRITICAL-THINKING PUZZLE

Without lifting your pencil from the paper, draw six straight lines that connect all sixteen of the dots below. To make things more challenging, the line pattern that you create must begin at the **X**.

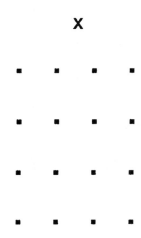

(The solution can be found at the end of this chapter.)

Source: DiSpezio, M. (1998). *Challenging critical thinking puzzles.* New York: Sterling.

Solution to Exercise 2

Critical-Thinking Puzzle

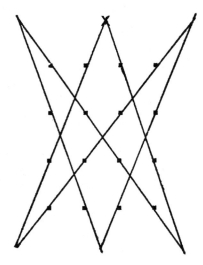

DiSpezio, M. (1998). *Challenging critical thinking puzzles.* New York: Sterling.

Chapter 9

Living in a World of Diversity

CASE STUDY

Kim

Kim has been diagnosed with multiple sclerosis and wears braces on both knees. Because she always wears pants, no one ever sees her braces, although sometimes it is difficult to walk. When Kim has to get to class on the 4th floor, she usually has a long wait for an available elevator. It is packed with able-bodied students who are not attuned to her disability. Many of them wouldn't even get off the elevator to make room for a student in a wheelchair.

Yoshi

Yoshi is Japanese-American. He is athletic and very interested in all kinds of sports, especially football. His teammates give him a hard time because he doesn't fit their idea of a football player. They expect him to know martial arts and help them with their homework. Throughout his school experience, teachers and students alike expected Yoshi to be a good math, science, and computer student.

Chris

Chris is a member of the Gay-Straight Alliance Club on campus. Last semester a poster announcing the club's meeting times was defaced with hateful messages. A few weeks later there was an anonymous letter to the editor in the school newspaper denouncing funding for their club. Chris is beginning to feel a distinct homophobic climate on campus and is wondering how best to deal with it.

Helen

Helen never thought she would be in this position. After years of taking care of her husband and raising her family, she now finds herself widowed with very little income. She needs to prepare for a job that will provide a good salary and benefits and will allow her to find employment as quickly as possible. She met with a workforce development specialist who is urging her to enter the health care field and earn a CNA (Certified Nurse Assistant) Certificate due to the shortage of nursing home workers. Helen is not particularly attracted to that field. In fact, she took some aptitude tests that showed above-average ability in mechanical/electrical occupations.

Reflections

- If you are an able-bodied person, how can you become more aware of and sensitive to students with physical limitations?
- What kinds of racial stereotypes are evident in Yoshi's story?
- What are the consequences of a negative campus climate for those who are discriminated against? For the rest of the campus?
- How did the workforce development specialist's attitude affect Helen's options?

INTRODUCTION

If you live and attended high school in a small, suburban, or rural community, you may be encountering more diversity at your college than you've ever experienced in your life. If you are from an urban environment, you may find your campus has more, less, or about the same amount of diversity that you are used to. Whichever the case may be, your future will include living, working, and doing business with people from all walks of life. They may be from different racial/ethnic/cultural groups, practice different religions, have a different social or economic status, speak different languages, be different ages, have physical/mental disabilities, have different sexual orientations, or work/be training for jobs that are not traditionally held by people of their gender. The ability to cooperate and work effectively with all types of people is an important skill that you need to develop in order to be successful in today's world.

Pretest

Answer yes or no to the following items:

	Yes	No
1. It is easier for minority students to get financial aid to attend college.	_____	_____
2. Discrimination against women and minorities in the workplace is a thing of the past.	_____	_____
3. The large middle class in the U.S. controls most of the nation's wealth.	_____	_____
4. Gay men/lesbian women are attracted to all members of the same sex.	_____	_____
5. Latino people don't want to learn English.	_____	_____
6. Victims of domestic abuse would leave their abusers if they really wanted to do so.	_____	_____
7. Asian students have higher GPAs than students of other cultural groups.	_____	_____

8. Older people are less productive in the workplace. _____ _____

9. Homeless people could easily change their situations
   if they tried. _____ _____

10. It is unlikely that I (or a member of my immediate family)
    will become disabled. _____ _____

You may have noticed that all of the statements on this pretest are false. They represent some commonly-held beliefs that are based on stereotypes rather than facts. In this chapter we will take a closer look at some of the *myths about diversity* as we provide you with some truths. You will read about the *population of the United States and how it is changing*. We will discuss the *"big three" diversity issues—race, social class, and gender*—that have been part of the historical legacy of discrimination in this country. Then, we will consider some of the *newer issues such as ability, age, and other forms of prejudice*. Finally, we will talk about some ways to *manage living and working in such a diverse society. Understanding intercultural communication patterns, deciding what is fair, and showing respect and acceptance for our fellow human beings* are all vital to our living in and contributing to a healthy society.

THE AMERICAN POPULATION

The Way It Was

When we look at the United States today, we see the results of hundreds of years of history. Who runs the country politically and economically, who gets along with whom, and what actions receive what kinds of reactions all come from the foundations that were laid when this nation was formed.

Aside from the Native Americans and Mexicans (a blend of Native Americans, Spanish, and Africans), most people coming to the New World were from the countries of northern and western Europe. At the time of the American Revolution, there was also a considerable population of people brought from Africa as slaves. In the 1800s immigrants from China, who came to work on the railroads, were populating the Pacific Coast states, especially California. By the early 1900s, the migration of people from western Europe gave way to an influx of immigrants from eastern and southern Europe.

As each new group of "foreigners" entered the country in sizeable numbers, many of those already established here became apprehensive, and in many instances, engaged in discriminatory actions. Fears that the new immigrants would take their jobs, intermarry with their children, speak languages they didn't understand, practice different religions, and bring strange, "un-American" ways of doing things to their communities fueled feelings of "us" versus "them." Newcomers were often unwelcome in established neighborhoods, and ethnic areas sprang up in most cities. In the late 1800s and early 1900s, laws were passed to limit the number of "undesirable" immigrants, such as the Chinese and Japanese, from entering the country. Many of these laws were not repealed until the mid-1960s.

Slavery was yet another matter. Although the slaves were freed after the Civil War, extreme prejudice and fear led many states and communities to pass laws that systematically discriminated against people of color, especially Blacks. It was illegal for slaves to be educated or own property, and even after slavery ended, they were often denied opportunities and rights that were taken for granted by other citizens.

The Way It Is

This history still affects all of us living in the United States today. The legacy of discrimination persists, and thus, we find ourselves dealing with problems in the twenty-first century that had their roots in the seventeenth, eighteenth, nineteenth, and twentieth centuries. One of the critical issues facing our nation today is whether we will be able to solve our dilemma concerning diversity. School curricula have long ignored the contributions of people of color in the sciences, math, history, literature, the arts, etc. Consequently, generations of Americans have grown up thinking that most of the knowledge of the world has come from white European cultures. This promotes feelings of superiority among some Euro-Americans.

The white majority has also controlled governments and the court systems at the local, state, and federal levels. Those in power influence the kinds of laws that are passed, the way they are interpreted, and the way they are enforced. Issues such as racial profiling and hate crimes dominate the news, signifying that Americans still struggle with how to get along. Terrorism is on the rise and has directly affected our country, resulting in fear, negative attitudes, and violent acts against innocent people who are targeted just because they come from the same ethnic background as the suspected terrorists. The problem will not go away by itself; indeed, it is far too important to ignore.

The Way It Will Be

There is no doubt that the population of the United States is getting more diverse. The 2000 census revealed some major demographic shifts in our country. For all of our nation's history, the dominant group numerically, politically, and economically has been Americans of European descent, most of whom classify themselves as "White, Non-Hispanic." In the next 100 years this will change. Predictions based on previous and current U.S. census data indicate that the number of White, Non-Hispanic people will steadily decrease each decade of this century. Sometime between 2055 and 2060, there will be a break-even point where the number of White, Non-Hispanics will fall to 50% of the total population. By the end of the twenty-second century, they will comprise about 40% of the population.

At the same time, the number of Hispanics will continue to increase. They were the second largest minority group throughout the 1990s, with slightly under 12% of the population in the 2000 census. By 2100, Hispanics are expected to become a third of the total population. Blacks, at 12.1% in the 2000 census, have previously been the largest minority group in the U.S. Their population is expected to stay very stable for the next hundred years, increasing to about 13% of the population at the end of the century.

Another group that is expected to grow rapidly is the Asian/Pacific Islanders. They comprised fewer than 4% of the population in 2000. Their numbers are expected to grow consistently each decade throughout this century. By 2100 they will almost match the number of Blacks living in the U.S. These projections are illustrated in Table 8.1.

The United States conducts a census of all citizens and residents living in the country every ten years. The categories above are those identified in the 2000 census. Further information can be obtained from the Census Bureau Web site at *www.census.gov.*

Implications for Change

If you are in your late teens and twenties and live into your 80s—which is quite likely, given the advances in health care—you will see this shift in population in your lifetime. But we don't have to wait that long to confront the issues that increased diversity will bring. Each new development in technology—radio, telephones, television, air travel, satellites, computers—brought the people of the world closer together. The introduction of the Internet cemented the relationship among us as customers in a global marketplace. Time and distance have lost their ability to control trade and productivity. Any possibility of isolationism on the part of the United States ended early in the twentieth century. International business is the norm, whether you are on the plains of central Iowa, the tundra of northern Alaska, the beaches of Florida, or in a major metropolitan area.

Table 8.1 PERCENT OF TOTAL POPULATION								
	2000	2010	2020	2030	2040	2050	2075	2100
White Non-Hispanic	71.4	67.3	63.8	60.1	56.3	52.8	45.6	40.3
Hispanic	11.8	14.6	17.0	19.4	21.9	24.3	29.5	33.3
Black Non-Hispanic	12.2	12.5	12.8	13.0	13.1	13.2	13.2	13.0
Asian/Pacific Islander	3.9	4.8	5.7	6.7	7.8	8.9	11.0	12.6
American Indian	0.7	0.8	0.8	0.8	0.8	0.8	0.8	0.7

Source: Projections of the Resident Population by Race, Hispanic Origin and Nativity, U.S. Census Bureau, Population Division, Washington, D.C.

How can we relate with the rest of the world, though, when we have not yet mastered the ability to get along with our fellow citizens? In the cities and states where demographic shifts have already taken place, people struggle with accepting differences. Many fear change. Others fear that people who look "different" will harm them or take away their quality of life. Some individuals/groups do not want to give up their privileges (or perceived privileges) so that others who are not part of their group may benefit. Although these thoughts and feelings are kept under control most of the time, one incident is often all it takes for old prejudices and stereotypes to surface.

THE BIG THREE: RACE, CLASS, AND GENDER

The concepts included in any discussion about diversity may be many and varied, but the three major areas of concern have always been—and still are—race, social class, and gender. Let's take a look at each one.

The Question of Race

How many races do you think there really are? If your answer is more than one, we all have a problem. How did this notion that there is more than one race, the human race, come into existence? Biologically/genetically, human beings are all of the same species. Regardless of skin/eye/hair color, language spoken, religion practiced, or cultural background, we can give each other our blood, transplant organs from one person to another, reproduce off-spring, etc. So, what purpose do you think it served to create a system that divided people into separate races? Who gained and who lost with such a system? Why do we perpetuate this type of classification? Why does racism (especially between Blacks and Whites) continue to be one of the nation's most prevalent social problems almost 150 years after slavery ended?

What do you think will happen when there is no longer one clear majority group? Will we all truly be equal then? Will we finally be able to overcome the divisiveness caused by years of living in a system that classifies people according to certain physical characteristics? Where do **you** stand on this issue?

If you identify yourself as a member of the white race, you are already in the smallest minority of people populating the earth. Does it bother you that within your lifetime, and certainly that of your children, the white population will be a minority in the United States? Are you able to live and work comfortably with the diversity of people around you? Do you understand that you benefit daily from unearned privilege just because of your skin color, and can you understand the frustration of those who have not been granted that same privilege?

If you consider yourself Hispanic or Latino, you are in one of the fastest growing groups worldwide. Historically, your group has always been underrepresented politically in the United States because many Latinos do not vote or get involved with politics. Male and female Latino students drop out of high school at much higher rates than their peers. Latinas (females) are among those least likely to attend college and finish a degree. Are you prepared to step up and take your place in society? Do you plan to finish college, earn a professional degree, and make sure that your children do the same?

If you are Black or African-American, you are living out the legacy that your parents and grandparents fought to achieve. Their sacrifices and persistence in the face of overwhelming obstacles earned you the right to attend the college of your choice, to shop in any store, to eat in whatever restaurant you choose, and to work alongside other Americans. Yet, their fear is that you will sit back complaisantly and stop the progress for which their generation worked so hard. They fear that you will give in to the myth that to be intelligent and accomplished in anything except music or sports is to "sell out" or "act white." Are you committed to stopping the cycle of poverty and hopelessness that fills the inner cities of America?

If you identify yourself as Asian/Pacific Islander, you may not see as many people in the United States with your physical features, but you are in the largest population group in the world. The prevailing stereotype is that all Asian-Americans are "A" students and are good in math, science, and with computers. It is true that for many years U.S. immigration policies primarily allowed scientists, doctors, and technologists to come to this country. It is also true that in many Asian families, education is highly valued; doing homework is a top priority. However, for those of you who are interested in athletics, social sciences, or fine arts, it may be frustrating not to be given the opportunity to do your thing because you are expected to be a math whiz or computer genius. This reaction was what Yoshi from our case studies at the beginning of the chapter experienced. As your population increases in the U.S., you should gain more visibility in all areas: government, media, athletics, business, etc. Are you fulfilling your personal goals and being true to yourself?

Many Americans do not identify with any of the groups listed above. A "multiracial" classification was added to the census for the first time in 2000. That made it easier for people with multiple heritages to feel included. (Counting and classifying has come a long way from the first census where the only choices were "White" and "Non-White.") Most Americans of Middle Eastern descent identify themselves as White because there is no category that accurately describes them. When you consider how rapidly this group is growing, you realize that the white population of European descent is shrinking faster than the population projections imply.

Native Americans must prove that they are at least 1/16 blood-related to a specific tribe in order to legally claim that heritage. Although they are the first Americans, Native American Indians were driven from their lands and denied a voice in American government. The attempt to systematically destroy their culture, language, and religion resulted in a legacy of poverty and addiction. In recent decades, however, there has been a resurgence of pride in their heritage, as well as general interest in Native American culture.

Assigning a racial identity to people is a tricky undertaking at best. Perhaps the real solution to the question of race is to view yourself as a member of the human race. Then, you will see the differences between human beings as surface variations among your neighbors, friends, and family.

Social Class

One characteristic that has made the United States such a great nation is that the middle class comprises the majority of the population. We don't have a large peasant class ruled by an aristocracy or a select group of military leaders. However, in the last half of the twentieth century, some of the progress made by the middle class was lost. Although the per capita income of Americans had increased, when the figures were adjusted for inflation, there was actually a decline in quality of life and income of the middle and lower classes. The gains reflected an increase in the incomes of the upper class. If we were to illustrate the distribution of wealth in the United States, it would look like an inverted pyramid with the wealthiest 10% of the population controlling 80% of the country's monetary resources. So, the rich really are getting richer, and the poor are getting poorer.

This is a cause for concern for all classes because the middle class is the only one that cannot pass its class status to the next generation. Children of upper class parents can inherit the family fortune and remain in the upper class. Poor parents have little material wealth to leave their children, which often leads to multi-generational poverty. That's why the middle class has always valued education as its primary means of holding on to its position or getting ahead. If children of middle class parents do not have sufficient skills to get good jobs and succeed on their own after reaching adulthood, they will not be able to maintain middle class status without support. With few exceptions, education level is directly related to income level. Statistically, people with higher levels of education also earn higher incomes.

With an increase in income level and social class comes better access to health care, hence, longer life expectancy. The opportunities available to you are also affected by income. Even personal safety is determined to some extent by where you can afford to live. In this country your quality of life is determined largely by your socio-economic status.

The good news is there was a slight decrease in the number of people and families living in poverty in the United States in 2000. The United States Census Bureau calculates the poverty index by comparing a family's income to its size. People whose household income is less than the threshold for the size of their family are said to be living in poverty. The poverty threshold for a family of four in 2000 was $17,463, and for an individual under the age of 65 it was $8,959.

Table 8.2

RACE/ETHNICITY	% LIVING IN POVERTY
All races	11.3
White Non-Hispanics	7.5
Blacks	22.1
Hispanics	21.2
Asian/Pacific Islander	10.8

The bad news is that poverty continues to be a reality for many, even in one of the wealthiest nations on Earth. Race/ethnicity is still a major factor in determining who is poor. Table 8.2 shows the percentage of people living below the poverty level in the United States in the year 2000 according to the Census Bureau.

Poverty is also highly related to marital status and gender. Women who are divorced or widowed often face poverty because their income has been dramatically reduced. This happened to Helen. She did not have a career prior to getting married and her lack of marketable skills made it difficult for her to earn a living wage. All women should be prepared to support themselves in case the need arises.

Single women with children are much more likely to be poor than married couples with children, single men with children, or unrelated individuals. Look at Table 8.3, which includes poverty levels of families in general and those headed by single females with children. Do you see the dramatic increase in poverty levels for single mothers and children?

Table 8.3 PERCENT OF PEOPLE LIVING BELOW THE POVERTY LEVEL

RACE/ETHNICITY	ALL PEOPLE	PEOPLE IN FAMILIES	SINGLE MOTHERS AND CHILDREN
All races	11.3	9.6	27.9
White Non-Hispanics	7.5	5.5	18.0
Blacks	22.1	20.8	38.7
Hispanics	21.2	20.1	36.5
Asian/Pacific Islander	10.8	9.5	19.5

Source: Historical Poverty Tables, U.S. Census Bureau

One of the newest faces of poverty in the twenty-first century is that of the young child. Homeless families now outnumber homeless singles. According to the National Coalition for the Homeless, families are the fastest growing segment of the homeless population. Over 1.2 million U.S. children are homeless on any given night, and 41% of these children are under the age of 5. The average age of the homeless population is 9 years old! What future consequences will there be for education, job training, and work-related issues for these young people? Over half of them switch schools at least two times during the year, and almost a fourth must repeat a grade because of it.

Poverty and homelessness go hand-in-hand. The federal government defines affordable housing as being about 30% of a person's income. Under that guideline, a minimum wage worker would have to work more than 80 hours per week in order to pay rent on the average two-bedroom apartment. For those whose income is not sufficient to pay for food, child care, health care, education, and housing, the latter is often the one that gets sacrificed or forfeited. Many people, even in the middle class, are living from paycheck to paycheck. An accident, major illness, or other unplanned expense is all it would take for them to lose their home.

The more factors you have working against you, the harder it is to become successful in American society. Because public schools are usually funded by property tax revenue, those located in poor areas lack the resources of their more affluent neighbors. They cannot afford the best teachers, equipment, or supplies. New technology is limited or sometimes even nonexistent. Graduates of these schools may be as intelligent and have as much or more potential to learn, but score lower on achievement tests than their peers who have benefited from numerous advantages. Consequently, they may not be accepted into the best colleges/universities or offered the same opportunities for career advancement. For years our society has struggled with how to make life more equitable and just for those whose educational and/or life experiences have not prepared them adequately. Affirmative action, busing, and other such programs have tried to bridge the gap, but are often criticized as being unfair or falsely held to cause reverse racism and/or classism.

The federal government created financial aid programs to help people in the low and middle economic classes attend college. Post-secondary education (college or vocational/ skills training) that prepares students for careers paying decent wages is the most cost-effective way to help people get out of or stay out of poverty. It may seem like minority students get financial aid at disproportionate rates compared to white students, but the facts show that minority students are more likely to come from families living below the poverty level. That explains why they are more likely to get government grants that are based on family income. The government does not request or require an applicant to indicate race or ethnicity on the FAFSA (Free Application for Federal Student Aid) forms. Privately funded scholarships do exist for minority students, but their numbers are not even close to the numbers of scholarships awarded to white students.

Gender

Historically, the first discrimination was probably between men and women. This phenomenon was already present at the beginning of our great nation. It is evidenced in the Preamble of the Constitution of the United States, when our forefathers emphasized that all men were created equal. That is literally what they meant—all **men**. (However, remember that in 1776 all men really meant all white, educated, male property owners.) The inequity was also evidenced by the more than 140 years it took women to finally get the right to vote and hold public office. This second-class status is socialized within the very fabric of our nation and its people. We are still trying to overcome the notion that women are the weaker gender.

It is very apparent when one looks at the inequities found within careers and salaries. If you take women in business as an example, we find that less than five women are Chief Executive Officers of the Fortune 500 companies (the 500 companies that make the most money in the U.S.). That means the other 99% of CEOs are men. In many instances, males still make more money than women for the same jobs with the same educational level. Even though it is illegal to discriminate in this manner, the practice continues. It is carefully concealed, but in jobs where there is not a straight scale, where negotiation is part of the starting salary process, men usually negotiate better deals than women. Why? It could be that women lack the confidence to drive a hard bargain, or it could be due to the person who does the hiring. More often than not, the person in charge of personnel selection is a man.

Even today when we know that most single-parent families are headed by women, and in most two-parent families, both spouses work outside the home, there is still the perception that men are the "breadwinners" and, therefore, should earn more. Think of how many men you know who feel threatened when their wives' salaries are higher than their own. Are they proud of her, or do they feel intimidated? How many couples would move to another city because the wife was offered a better job?

Yet, although they earn less, women pay more for goods and services. When women buy cars, they pay inflated prices compared to men. They are charged more for services such as dry cleaning clothes, alterations, haircuts, and car or home repairs. Women are also more likely to be victims of domestic violence and physical assault. Many women stay in abusive relationships out of fear and because they lack alternative means to support themselves and their children. Anti-stalking laws and orders of protection do not prevent a woman from becoming a victim. These laws can only be enforced after a crime has been committed and, even then, are often violated and not consistently enforced.

In government we still see inequities between men and women despite all of our progress. As of this writing, there are eight governors, fourteen United States senators, and two women on the Supreme Court. However, inasmuch as women make up 51% of the population, that's still gross under-representation. Women win elections at about the same rate as men when neither is an incumbent (person currently doing the job). Male and female incumbents win elections at a much higher rate than challengers. The few women in elected positions show not that people won't elect women, but that women are still playing catch-up for all the years they were prevented from holding elected positions. There are far more male incumbents today because there have always been more males in office.

In the career arena we find the major professions traditionally held by women do not have the earning power of male-dominated occupations. We've all heard the argument that women tend to work at less demanding, less difficult occupations, that their jobs take less skill and expertise than male dominated occupations. Is it really true that the person who cares for your child or teaches your child to read is worth less per hour than the person who unclogs your sink or hauls away your garbage? Studies indicate that in 2003 women's earnings for year-round, full-time employment were 75.5% of men's salaries. In almost every occupation, though, you will find a wage gap between men's and women's salaries even when they are doing the same job. We could try to explain this by saying that men have worked longer in these occupations, and therefore, have more experience. But that won't explain why men in traditionally female occupations such as administrative assistants, nurses, and elementary school teachers continue to have higher salaries.

Sometimes the issues are not as obvious. Bias can be found in something as subtle as providing less funding for medical research to cure breast cancer or other "women's diseases." It can be a teacher giving girls in class less encouragement to pursue higher levels of math and science. In fact, studies done by Drs. David and Myra Sadker showed that elementary and secondary school teachers gave more instruction and attention to the boys in their classes than the girls, even when the teachers were aware that they were being studied and were trying to be equitable. Girls were praised more often for their appearance and the neatness of their work. If they made mistakes, they were told that they were incorrect but not given further instruction. Boys in the same classrooms were praised more for the quality of their work, and when they made mistakes, they were retaught the concept.

The Sadkers also studied the students' self-concepts. They found that girls had higher self-concepts and expectations of success than boys in elementary school and junior high, but by the time they reached high school, the boys far outpaced the girls in those same areas. The study concluded that the socialization process still tells girls that there are limits to what they can achieve and that it's not feminine to be smart in science, math, technology, and/or the skilled trades.

DIVERSITY ISSUES TODAY

We've come a long way toward acknowledging that prejudice and injustice stifled the opportunities of many Americans in the past. Making the connection between that historical legacy and current problems is more difficult for many students to see. However, we live in an age of international businesses where companies are bought and merged with others across continents, and chances are you will work for and with people who are very different from you. If you can't get along in a diverse workforce, you will find your employment opportunities severely limited. It is time for each of us to confront our own attitudes and beliefs. Ask yourself, "How well will I be able to cope if my boss and/or co-workers speak another language, practice a different religion, come from a 'foreign' culture, have a different sexual orientation, are much older/younger than me, or are disabled?"

Ability

How do you react when you see someone in a wheelchair? Do you ignore him/her or look away? Do you think of him/her as less intelligent? If she/he is with a companion, do you speak to the person directly or to the companion? Do you act like she/he is also hard of hearing or cannot speak? These are common reactions that people with disabilities experience constantly. Since 1990 there has been a federal law giving those with disabilities a chance for equal opportunities. If you have ever had to use crutches or a wheelchair for a period of time, you may have a slight appreciation for what persons with physical disabilities experience on a daily basis. Trying to engage in normal activities such as using public restrooms, sitting in a theater, boarding an airplane, train, or bus, shopping for groceries, or attending a sporting event can be quite an ordeal. As an able-bodied person, do you resent having to walk farther because the parking spaces closest to the door are designated handicapped? Do you step aside or use the stairs when a person in a wheelchair or someone in braces (such as Kim in our case study) is waiting to get on a crowded elevator?

What if the disability is not obvious? What about someone with a learning disability? Do you think it is a waste of taxpayer money to fund special tutorial programs for L.D. (learning disabled) students? What if you are the person with a learning disability? Many students with learning disabilities have had to endure years of suffering because parents, teachers, and classmates didn't understand their disability and accommodate them. Schools today try to do a better job identifying these students at an early age, but if you are an adult, you may not have been so fortunate.

Our culture seems to value people according to two main criteria: physical attractiveness (beauty/youth) and intelligence. In his book, *Hide or Seek*, psychologist Dr. James Dobson calls them the gold and silver coins of self-worth. Those people blessed with the golden coin of beauty usually don't have a problem finding friends and getting positive attention from others. From the time they are cute babies through their high school years when appearance is the key to popularity, they seem to draw people in with their good looks and charming smiles. Those with the silver coin, intelligence, may not be as popular as their golden classmates, but they, too, are recognized as possessing something of great value. Their parents and teachers are proud of them; they win awards; they feel good about themselves and what they can accomplish.

Let's turn the picture over, though, and look at some of the other children. Imagine a child with a learning disability who cannot understand the lessons the way his/her teacher explains them. She/he receives no awards for outstanding performance, even though she/he may put forth much greater effort to learn. What is done to rescue the self-esteem of this student? The child with a physical disability is often made to feel less than adequate in a society that worships perfection. Do we contribute to these problems with our perceptions of people with disabilities? Do we limit the things we think they can accomplish?

This is another area where we might really need to make some adjustments in our thinking. Sometimes life has a way of forcing us to rethink and adjust our attitudes. People who are able-bodied and perfectly healthy one day can, through an accident or illness, become disabled in a matter of minutes. The chance of developing some type of disability in your lifetime is 50%, and that percentage increases as you age. What will you do then? Will you give up on yourself, or will you continue to achieve, excel, and enjoy life?

We have many examples of people who have overcome extreme disabilities and accomplished great feats. Some have done more with their lives because of their disabilities than they would have had they stayed able-bodied. One example is a woman named Joni Erickson Tada. As a result of a diving accident when she was a teenager, Joni became a quadriplegic who has no control over her body from the neck down. During rehabilitation therapy she learned to paint by holding the paintbrush with her teeth. After she became well known for her art, she decided to tell her story in a book. That was the beginning. Today, she has written several books, has had two movies made about her life story, has become an international authority and advocate for the disabled, is invited to speak at conferences around the world, runs her own charitable corporation, and has a daily radio program.

Probably we can all think of someone who has not let a physical or learning disability keep them from achieving success. Some of the greatest scientists, musicians, artists, entertainers, politicians, and athletes have had to overcome seemingly impossible odds to accomplish their goals.

Age

Ageism may have been around for quite a while, but it is receiving considerable attention now that the baby-boom generation is getting older. Advances in health care have enabled people to be productive into their later years. Many choose to continue working in their careers because they find their work stimulating and satisfying. Some pursue a new career after retirement to keep themselves busy and active. On the other hand, the economic situation of many older Americans is what keeps them in the workforce. They simply cannot afford to retire.

At the same time, our workplaces are changing. Technology, information, and innovations are constantly forcing companies to keep up. They seek younger, energetic workers who can deal with constant change and who are knowledgeable about the latest technology. Older workers can find themselves devalued and pushed aside. As a culture and as individuals, we seem to have lost respect for our elders. We're too busy to sit and talk with them and learn from their wisdom. Their slowness irritates us if it interferes with our faster pace.

However, those companies that do take advantage of hiring seniors find that they are excellent employees. Most were raised in a time when you had to have a good work ethic. They are dependable, hardworking, honest, and can save the company money because their absentee rate is much lower than younger workers, while their punctuality rate is much higher.

Of course, ageism can go the other way, too. Sometimes teenagers are the targets of negative stereotyping. Because of the widespread negative publicity about teens who commit crimes, people get the impression that all young people are lazy, selfish, troubled, and confused. The reverse is closer to the real truth. Teens today are doing better than those of previous generations in many ways.

Other "Isms" That Separate Us

Another step on our journey toward making this nation a more perfect union of people is to rid ourselves of the "isms." We've taken a look at the big three: racism, classism, and sexism. We've also discussed discrimination against people with disabilities and ageism. Unfortunately, there are still more dragons out there to slay. So, pick up your sword, and let's go get them!

What are some of the "isms" you've encountered? You may not be able to label them with snappy, one-word descriptions, but you know when you've observed or experienced them. Perhaps it is prejudice because of religious beliefs. What about discrimination based on a person's size? Have you ever noticed how people treat someone (especially a woman) who is very large, or someone (especially a man) who is very short? Those who don't fit the "norm" are likely to be ridiculed and rejected because they are different.

Cases involving harassment and discrimination against homosexuals have made news headlines in recent years. Homophobia—an extreme prejudice against gay men and/or lesbian women—causes those who fear homosexuals to act out against them. Behaviors ranging from "practical jokes" to assault or defamation violate the victim's civil rights and are inappropriate in any setting. Many corporations and municipalities have adopted policies aimed at protecting employees and preventing discrimination based on sexual orientation.

People with alternative lifestyles are a part of your campus and your community. Your campus may have a gay/lesbian club or organization. Gay/lesbian students are entitled to the same rights and considerations as all other persons on campus. Chris was right to be concerned about the negative campus climate he experienced. You will encounter people with different lifestyles wherever people are found—in the workplace, in your neighborhood, within organizations to which you belong, in your place of worship, etc.

Whenever we put another person into a category labeled "other" or "not like us," it increases the chances that we will treat them differently than we would like to be treated. It makes it easier to rationalize away behavior that we would immediately recognize as wrong if it happened to someone in our family. Watch for other examples of the "isms" as you interact with people. As we mentioned earlier, treat others as though you were one of them. Then, resolve to become part of the solution, not part of the problem. Become an advocate for justice, fairness, and equity through your own words and actions.

MANAGING WORKPLACE DIVERSITY

Intercultural Communication

Every encounter with another person is an intercultural exchange. We each see the world with perceptions developed from our own experiences. We've each developed a communication style that serves our needs. Misunderstandings arise, though, when our style clashes with another person's communication style. We think they are being emotional and unprofessional. They think we are cold and don't care enough about important issues. Suddenly there is a problem. What is the answer to dealing with people who are different when we all have to get along?

Dr. Milton Bennett has identified several sets of factors that make up a person's communication style. First, recognize your own style; then watch for these elements when you communicate with others. Recognizing that there are style differences can help you tune in to what your co-worker is really trying to say. For example, some people get right to the point when they talk. They might fill in a few details later, but the "bottom line" is what communication means to them. For other people, the context and the details are essential, and from there the listener can figure out the main point. To them it is condescending to spell everything out as you would to a young child. Imagine what happens in a business meeting where the participants have opposing styles. One person is thinking, "Why does she/he talk in circles? I don't need all of this information. This is a waste of time." The other person is thinking, "Does she/he think I'm stupid? Why won't she/he trust me with all of the details?"

In western cultures, communication tends to be very direct. You have probably heard someone say, "I just tell it like it is." Saying exactly what you're thinking, without worrying about whether or not the circumstances and timing are perfect is an approach many Americans use regularly. However, people in several Eastern cultures find directness rude and insulting, especially if the news is bad. They may favor a more indirect style where meaning is conveyed through nonverbal behavior and implications. Indirect communicators may make statements within earshot of the person intended to hear rather than address the comment directly to that person. This allows the listener to hear the message, but is far less confrontational.

Another difference in the way people communicate has to do with how much they depend on words and how much they say through nonverbal messages. Some people are very good at "reading between the lines," while others take everything that is said at face value. Men and women often have this style difference in personal relationships. She thinks he should understand without being told. Her internal dialog says, "If he was observant, he would know." His internal dialog says, "That's ridiculous. How am I supposed to know what she wants if she doesn't tell me?"

Establishing clear communication is extremely important in the business world where profits are made or lost by the way employees interact with customers and each other. Corporations spend millions of dollars on conflict resolution training. Many times this training involves personality testing that helps people understand themselves and their patterns of interacting. Recognizing that people have different personality types and communication styles makes one aware of how to interpret another's way of expressing him/herself. As you talk with others on the job, at the college, and in your personal life, try not to judge them or be offended if they don't respond the way you expect; instead approach the situation with an open mind. Different isn't necessarily better or worse; it's just different.

Deciding What Is "Fair"

How does an individual or an employer know which is the right way to proceed when making decisions that involve diversity? How can you be sure that you are being just or fair in your treatment of others? There are two ways of approaching the issue. Both have merit and work in many situations. Read through the two descriptions and decide which you favor instinctively. Then consider the other approach and think about the positives and negatives of using that. Be objective and open minded; think of situations when it might be better to switch from your preference to the other point of view.

The first approach is systematic and rule-based. One establishes policies and procedures for doing things and then follows them closely. Decisions are made by adhering to specific guidelines. Everyone is treated the same because the standards are the same for all. Companies with policies that apply to every employee from the entry-level workers to the executives are practicing this kind of fairness. If your college uses a placement test, the same cut-off scores should apply to all students. Parents who want to be fair often try to treat their children the same. If they buy something for one child, they buy something of equal value for the other children.

The second approach is not as rigid in its application. Sometimes following the rules too closely gets in the way of what makes sense in the situation. Taking extenuating circumstances into account and treating each person as an individual ensures fairness. Schools that have zero tolerance policies for drugs and weapons are under fire for suspending a student who gives a friend an aspirin or accidentally leaves a butter knife in the car. Companies may make an exception to a tardiness rule if an employee was late due to an auto accident on the way to work. Most parents wouldn't think of buying glasses for all of their children just because one child needs them or buying glasses for one child and gifts of equal value for the others.

In many situations you will be faced with deciding what is the best way to respond. Is it fairer to hold to the standard, or is it better to look at the unique circumstances and do what is best in the situation? When dealing with diversity, sometimes the second approach makes more sense. We are not all the same. A culturally sensitive person will look for clues and cues about how others prefer to be treated. There is not an instant answer; it may take time and effort to develop your intercultural skills.

Respect and Acceptance

In recent years we have seen people do terrible things to one another because they can't deal with their differences. How do we help them process their anger when dealing with someone who is different?

Many diversity programs emphasize tolerance. If we are all going to live and work together, we have to move beyond tolerance. One of the most positive ways to ensure workplace harmony is for us to treat each other with respect and acceptance. Recognize that we are better off because of our differences than we would be apart. Diversity isn't about others; it's about all of us.

If you struggle with issues of diversity, try the following tips for becoming a more open and accepting person.

- *Develop a sense of community.* When you interact with people in a friendly environment, you begin to feel part of the group. It is easier to support and understand someone with whom you have established a rapport or relationship. At work or at the college, try to eat lunch or take breaks with fellow employees/students whose backgrounds differ from yours.
- *Travel or participate in cultural exchanges.* This can give you the most amazing change of perspective. Seeing/hearing another country's news report makes you aware of the cultural bias in our own media. Meeting and talking with people on their "turf" helps you see things from their point of view.
- *Learn another language/learn about another culture.* Knowledge is power. If you lack knowledge about other cultures, take a cultural diversity course. Many colleges/universities insist that their students take at least one course from a different cultural perspective. Knowing a second language not only helps you communicate with people, but it is also a window into their culture.

- *Practice cultural humility.* Our own way of doing things may not always be the only way, the right way, or even the best way.

SUMMARY

Even though we like to think that every individual in the United States has an equal opportunity to achieve and succeed, the facts do not support that assumption. Some have a much greater head start. Factors such as parental levels of education and income, individual talent and skill, educational background, and opportunities/experiences contribute to a person's chance for success.

In this chapter we have explored a few of the many concepts of diversity. The changing population in the United States and the globalization of our economy are forcing Americans to deal with people who are different in a sensitive, just, and equitable way.

We considered the three biggest categories of diversity—race, social class, and gender— and how each of them has disadvantaged portions of our population. The new issues— ability, age, and other "isms"—were also discussed. To manage workplace diversity, learn how you communicate and understand that others may use a different style. Treat those you encounter with respect and acceptance.

To quote Dr. Milton Bennett, "The end result of a discussion on ethnicity should be to increase and celebrate it—that's diversity. The end result of a discussion on race should be to decrease the impact of it—that's unity."

CRITICAL THINKING ESSAY

Choose one of the following topics and write about it:

1. Think about an incident of discrimination or harassment that you experienced or witnessed. (The discrimination may have been based on race, ethnic group, religion, sex, physical disability, or age.) How did the experience affect you and the other person(s) involved? Discuss your feelings, values, beliefs, and actions after the incident. What actions can you take to reduce the occurrence of such incidents?

2. Reflect upon sex discrimination in our society. How has it affected you or a person who is important to you (e.g., your spouse, child, friend, or relative)? Write about the effect of sex discrimination on self-esteem, education, career choices, relationships, and leisure activities. What is your attitude about sex discrimination?

3. Write about the experiences of someone you know who has a physical or learning disability. How has that person coped with the challenges of daily life, pursuing his or her education, participating in leisure activities, establishing a social life, or finding a job?

4. If you are a non-traditional student (more than 25 years of age), write about the sources of support that have encouraged you to attend and succeed in college (e.g., your family, a mentor, a friend, your own inner strength and motivation). What additional resources might you tap to help you succeed in college? How have you coped with the challenge of juggling the many roles in your life in addition to your role as a student? How do you feel about being an older student on campus?

5. If you are a traditional college student (less than 25 years of age), write about your experiences with non-traditional students. How have they enhanced your college education? Are there any disadvantages to having non-traditional students on campus?

6. Are all of the buildings in which you attend classes and participate in meetings or activities handicapped accessible? If not, find out (a) why not and (b) what you can do to see that the necessary changes are made.

7. Are you currently volunteering at a homeless shelter or at a food pantry? If so, describe your experience.

8. Are you involved in mentoring disadvantaged students? If so, describe your experience and the program in which you are involved.

9. If you are not currently involved in any socially/educational voluntary activity, make a list of specific opportunities in your community.

NAME: _____ **DATE:** _____

EXERCISE 1.

Suppose you have to write a research paper for a sociology class. The paper has to be about diversity in the United States.

Step 1. Choose a topic on diversity. The following are a few suggested topics:

Age discrimination   Bilingual education

Discrimination in education   Discrimination in employment

Gay marriage/civil unions   Multicultural education

Racial/ethnic profiling   Social class

_____

Step 2. Write down keywords you can use for searching your topic. Also think about how they can be further refined: Discrimination in education (religious, gender, race for example). Also, keep in mind that location (United States) can help refine a search.

_____

Step 3. Use the computerized catalog system in your college's library/learning resource center and locate one reference book that you could use for your paper.

Name of book _____

Author(s)_____

Call number _____

Step 4. Using one of the periodical databases, identify three journal/magazine articles that would help you gather information for your paper. Print an *abstract* of each article and attach it to this page or copy down the full citation.

Article 1 _____

_____

_____

_____

_____

Article 2 _____

_____

_____

Article 3 _____

_____

_____

Step 5. Read one of the articles and be prepared to give a brief summary of it in class.

Appendix

1. University Vocabulary

A. Academic Advisor—person who is assigned to the student to discuss academic program requirements, campus resources, and regulations, course selection, plans/goals for the future.

B. Academic Freedom—includes faculty control of content and method of course delivery; ability to teach and learn without fear of reprisal.

C. Academic Integrity—scholarly honesty in research, publication, use of facilities and services, and use of one's rank.

D. Academic Dismissal (aka "drop")—removal from University for 1 regular semester. NOTE: 2.20 GPA required to return to the School of Management.

E. Blackboard—online course management system used to assist in teaching, testing and assignments, especially in distance learning courses.

F. Catalog—online book of all courses & depts. offerings; also regulations for University; faculty names and schooling history.

G. CODO—"change of degree objective" move from one college to another within PUC.

H. Co-requisite—course required to take with another.

I. Counselor—one who assists students in determining ways of solving problems or deliberates situations at the student's request.

J. Credit hour—unit that designates the value, level or tie requirements of an academic course. *In most cases*, usable for a degree.

K. CRN—Course Reference Number—a unique number assigned to individual class sections. They are listed on the online class schedule and needed for web registration.

L. Degree Works—a web-based application used by students and advisors to track progress toward a degree.

M. Experiential Learning—also known as EXL, is hands-on learning. Opportunities include, but are not limited to internships, student research, study abroad, service learning. All PUC students are required to have 2 EXL courses in order to graduate.

N. Freshman Year Experience—also known as FYE is a required course designed to assist and guide students in maximizing their potential for success at the University by promoting academic growth. Emphasis is placed on campus resources, goal setting, academic planning, and career exploration.

O. Full-time student—students are considered full time if they are taking at least 12 credit hours in a semester. Any number of credits below 12 is considered Part time.

P. Grade Point Average— GPA-Average of all grades earned @ Purdue; A = 4pts, A– = 3.667, B+ = 3.333, B = 3, B– = 2.667, C+ = 2.333, C = 2, C– = 1.667, D+ = 1/333, D = 1, D– = .667, F = 0.

Q. Hold—a restriction on a student's ability to register for classes.

R. Incomplete ("I")—grade that can be given if the student has completed half of the course, is passing at the time of the request, and is given permission by the professor of the course. A valid reason for not completing the course is required and is to be submitted to the professor for approval.

S. Intercampus Transfer—move from 1 Purdue campus to another; only 1 record & 1 GPA for each student for all campuses.

T. Major—an undergraduate's main field of study. Upper level courses usually taken junior & senior years.

U. Minor—(usually optional) a secondary area of study. Fewer upper level courses than a major.

V. Placement testing—results used to determine the proper placement of students in math, English or foreign languages. Students are enrolled in the appropriate courses based on the level of competency demonstrated through the tests.

W. Plagiarism—Representing another person's words or ideas as your own. This activity is in violation of University policy and could result in failure of a course or expulsion from the University.

X. Pre-requisite—Required course to be taken before another course.

Y. Probation—academic warning to improve grades or be dismissed from the University.

Z. PUID—**P**urdue **U**niversity **Id**entification number is a unique number assigned to all students, faculty and staff.

AA. Readmit—Student allowed to return on probation after acad. Drop; 2.20 GPA required to return to the School of Management.

BB. Reentry—stopped attending university for a period of 2 consecutive years but in good standing when stopped out. Degree requirements could change while student is gone. Student must follow the new program requirements. GPA of 2.20 required to return to the School of Management.

CC. SOM Repeat Policy—Courses specified on the plan of study can only be repeated 2 times. If not successful, student must move out of the School of Management for a period of 5 years.

DD. Semester—Spring or Fall 17 week academic term which includes spring and fall breaks as well as university recognized holidays falling with the start and end dates of the term. The last week of the semesters "finals week." Summer terms are shorter sessions with varying start and end dates. Summer terms are not considered semesters.

EE. Semester Index—Average of grades for 1 semester.

FF. Student Classification—based on # of hrs. that are applicable to declared degree. Changes every 15 hours.

GG. Supplemental Instruction—group help for specific class section of difficult course. "SI" has had class & passed it successfully.

HH. Transfer credit—courses accepted by PUC from another university—not all may be applicable to your degree.

II. Tutoring—individual or small group help with course work.

JJ. Undistributed (UND)Transfer Credit—course accepted at PUC but has no equal @ PUC; *may* be usable in degree—see major advisor.

KK. Withdrawal—removed from class by choice or administratively. The 12th week of a semester is the last week to voluntarily withdraw from a class.

Revised April, 2012

2. Decoding Your Syllabus

DIRECTIONS: Using the *hardest or most important class you are taking this semester* as the subject of this exercise, take out all the materials for that course: syllabus, class schedule, any handouts that tell you what you will be doing in the course. Then answer the following questions.

Course Information: _____Department_____ Number _____ Section_____

1. Does this class require attendance? _____

2. How many absences if any are excused? _____

3. Do you know of any classes you definitely will miss? _____

4. What is the policy regarding missed exams, assignments, quizzes?

5. How are grades computed in this course?

   Judging by the way the grades are computed, on which parts of the course should you work the hardest?

6. What are the important dates in this course? List exam dates, due dates for assignments and when they are due.

   Is there a final exam? _____ Is it cumulative? _____

   Find the time and date for the final in the Schedule of Classes.

   Date _____ Time _____

7. What aspects of this course will cause the most trouble? Check all that apply.

   Note taking   _____

   Writing assignments   _____

   Reading the text   _____

   Speaking in front of the class   _____

   Studying for exams   _____

   Participating in class discussions   _____

   Understanding basic concepts   _____

   Other   _____ Explain.

8. Is this course required for your degree? _____

   Is there a minimum grade required for this class? _____

   What is the minimum grade? _____

   Is this class a prerequisite to another course you must take for your degree? _____

9. Is there anything in the syllabus that you do not understand? _____

   What is it?

   Where can you get help to understand?

10. Describe below your overall strategy for doing well in this course.

11. WHAT IS YOUR INSTRUCTOR'S NAME? _____
    (Memorize it!!!)

12. WHAT ARE THE INSTRUCTOR'S OFFICE HOURS? _____

REVISED 4/12

3. Plan of Study Assignment Instructions

This exercise is designed to teach the student how to plan out his/her academic program. The student will pick a major and select the courses to be taken for that degree. The courses for the plan are to be projected out 5 semesters. It is not necessary to know if the courses are actually offered. It is only necessary to list courses needed for the degree in the order they should be taken.

Please consider spending time on this assignment to ensure that you receive as many points as possible. This assignment is worth 75 points.

1. Top portion of the form—your choice of degree (Ex: BS in Management, BS in Accounting, BS in Computer Information Systems, BA in Business, BA in Sociology or BA in Psychology) The degree must match your intended major. Use the date you are completing the chart.

2. First column—Subject and Course number—for example, **MGMT 20000**.

3. Second column— # Credits—for example, **3** credits (for MGMT 20000).

4. Third column—Pre-requisite—you are to list the pre-requisite class for the class listed in the SUBJ/CRSE# column. Example, **MA 15300** (for MGMT 20000, Psy 20300). If there is no pre-requisite, write "none".

5. Fourth Column—Course Title—**Introductory Accounting, Introduction to Psychology**.

6. Add up the total number of credit hours for each semester.

7. Where can you obtain the required information for columns 1–4?

    Answer! Course descriptions and class schedule that are both on the line under the "Student" tab on the University home page.

8. Attach a copy of your Plan of Study to this assignment.

HERE IS A SAMPLE:

NAME ___John Doe_____   BS OR BA ___BS Management, Accounting, etc.___

DATE _____10/30/12_____   INTENDED MAJOR ___Finance, Psychology, etc.___

Current Semester's courses ___Fall 2012___

SUBJ/CRSE #	# CREDIT/S	PRE-REQUISITE	COURSE TITLE
Engl 10400	3	HS grades/ELP or TOEFL	Engl Comp I
Mgmt 10000	1	None	Mgmt Lectures
Soc 10000	3	None	Intro to Sociology
Ma 15300	3	ALEKS score	ALG/TRIG 1
Mgmt 10100	3	None	Intro to Business
	13	TOTAL CREDIT HOURS FOR THIS SEMESTER	

9. <u>Items for inclusion in the "Notes" section:</u>
    a. Summer classes Place * between spring & fall term where you plan to take course/s
    b. Transfer credits Place * above the "Current semester" section
    c. Classes taken previously to this semester Place * above the "Current semester" section
    d. Placement test credit (ex. Foreign language or Math placement) Place * above the "Current semester" section
    e. Advanced Placement test credit from high school Place * above the "Current semester" section
    f. Dual credits from high school Place * above the "Current semester" section
    g. CLEP credits Place * above the "Current semester" section
    h. Any other special information pertinent to this assignment
    i. If you are changing schools within PUC or transferring to another school, please attach your new plan of study (bingo sheet) to this assignment

10. **Please note: you cannot take a pre-requisite class in the same semester as the class that requires the pre-requisite** (for example, MA 15300 and MGMT 20000 cannot be taken in the same semester; you must take MA 15300 in one semester and MGMT 20000 or for Psych majors, PSY 20300 in the next semester).

11. For Bachelor of Science degree in Management or in the Bachelor of Science in Accounting, you should concentrate on taking your pre-management courses first before going on to upper (300+) level classes.

12. For most BA degrees, you should concentrate on taking your pre-business courses first before going on to the rest of your courses. For Behavioral Science majors, it is important to complete your English, foreign language and math requirements as soon as possible.

13. Some classes may have a class restriction (OBHR 33000 and MGMT 30100 or PSY 48000 and SOC 30700). In these examples, you need to have a junior classification (Class 5 means at least 61 credit hours attained). You can add up the total number of credit hours earned per semester to see if you meet this requirement.

14. The maximum number of credits allowable for one semester is 18 without special permission.

15. Any questions before turning in this assignment? Please ask your freshman course instructor.

16. **Hint:** It is easier to plan out the courses needed if the student has the Plan of Study or the list of degree requirements for the intended major.

4. Plan of Study Assignment

Name: _____   BS or BA _____

Date _____   Intended Major _____

Current Semester's Courses _____

SUBJ/CRSE #	# CREDIT/S	PRE-REQUISITE #	COURSE TITLE

Total CREDIT Hours for this Semester

Semester 2 _____

SUBJ/CRSE #	# CREDIT/S	PRE-REQUISITE #	COURSE TITLE

Total CREDIT Hours for this Semester

Semester 3 _____

SUBJ/CRSE #	# CREDIT/S	PRE-REQUISITE #	COURSE TITLE

Total CREDIT Hours for this Semester

Semester 4 _____

SUBJ/CRSE #	# CREDIT/S	PRE-REQUISITE #	COURSE TITLE

Total CREDIT Hours for this Semester

Semester 5 _____

SUBJ/CRSE #	# CREDIT/S	PRE-REQUISITE #	COURSE TITLE

Total CREDIT Hours for this Semester

Notes: _____

_____

_____

_____

_____

_____

_____

_____

_____

_____

_____

REVISED 4/12

5. Tips and Questions for the Interview for Information

Tips for conducting the Interview for Career Information:

- Select at least two persons who may be able to provide you with the time and who have the experience in the career you want to pursue.
- Call the person/s to make an appointment for about 1 hour. Inform him/her that the **purpose of your interview** is to complete a class assignment, **NOT** to apply for a job. Make sure you have your planner with you when you make the call so you have your availability in front of you.
- Be sure to allow the person you are interviewing to offer his/her availability first and then see if you can fit it into yours.
- Be sure to confirm your appointment the day before by calling the person or his/her secretary.
- On the day of the interview, dress appropriately. Dress professionally, as if you already hold the job; or if you are not able to do this, then dress as neatly as you would for a special occasion.
- Be polite and defer to the person you are interviewing.
- Make sure to let the person know that you will be taking notes about what is said so that you can write your paper.
- You can ask all the questions listed below or those that seem appropriate. Make sure you gather enough information to write a comprehensive paper. Let the person talk freely. He/she may give you more information than what is being asked. It can be more helpful in writing your paper if you use your active listening skills. Remember you are *seeking information only*.
- Be sure to shake hands and thank the person for his/her time and knowledge.
- Follow up with a thank you letter, <u>in business format</u>. Express how the person helped you. See example on next page.

Suggested Interview for Career Information Questions:

- What is a typical workday like in your job?
- What is the most rewarding part of this job?
- Is there company training necessary for this job? What does the training entail?
- How would you describe the ideal candidate for an entry level job leading to your level? What talents are needed at the entry level for this career?
- How would you describe both the physical and psychological working environment?
- Where does the job you hold fit into the company as a whole? Who is your supervisor? Are you required to work with a team or is most of your work done individually?
- Is professional growth encouraged? Is there room for advancement within the company?
- How long do people stay with this company/agency? Is there a lot of turnover? Do they move to new jobs within or do they have to go to other companies/agencies in order to advance in their career?

- What part of the job is most challenging? Why?
- If you could, what would you change about your job? Why?
- What are the strengths that a person needs to do this job successfully?
- How much travel or overtime is expected? Is it constant, seasonal, or occasional?
- Is this career more analytical or more people oriented or both?
- How is performance feedback or review conducted? By whom and how often?

6. Sample Business Letter in Block Style

1
2
3
4
5
6
7
8
9
10 Month, Day, Year
1
2
3
4
5 spaces
Name of person interviewed
Title of Person
Company Name
Company Address
City, State, Zip Code

Dear Mr./Ms. Interviewee' Name:

Body of letter to include thank you for the interview and their time. State what you learned in the interview and how you will use it for your assignment and if or how the information will help you in the future.

Restate your gratitude for their help and their support of you.

Sincerely,
1
your signature here
3
4spaces
Type your full name
Street address
City, State, Zip code

NOTE: *The letter should be centered on the page, equidistant from the top and bottom of the page.*

REVISED 4/12

7. Final Portfolio Project

The idea of this project is to develop a comprehensive package that displays usable information about you as a person, your educational plan, and your goals for the future. By pulling together some of the activities and homework assignments that you have completed during the semester, and doing some additional research into your career, you will have created your own roadmap. This portfolio is to be assembled in the following order in a folder that is clean and professional looking. <u>Appearance and presentation count</u>.

PORTFOLIO CONTENTS

1. Title Page: Project Title; the course number/section; course title; instructor's name; student's name
2. Contents Page listing the Sections and their contents, including page numbers
3. Section 1: "It's All About Me"
   a. Essay (full page <u>minimum</u> with margins of 1 inch on top and bottom, font size 11) on who I am now versus who I was on the first day of college. What have I learned about myself?
   b. Homework: Learning Styles Assignment
4. Section 2: My Educational Plan
   a. Plan of Study Homework Assignment

   Plan of Study or a sheet stating transfer to another University or training program or job.
   b. Copy of upcoming semester's class registration
5. Section 3: My Future
   a. Essay on "Why I selected this career" (1 full page <u>minimum </u>with margins of 1 inch top and bottom, font size 11) to include:
      i.   Your plan to reach your career goal stating:
           Experiential learning opportunities available

           Part time work that will enhance your opportunities

           A list of post graduate degrees or certifications or training necessary to advance in your career
      ii. Current information regarding job prospects and *entry level salaries* for this career.
   b. Career Research Homework Assignment
   c. *Interview for Information* (2 full page minimum with margins of 1 inch on top and bottom, font size 11). Must be a person you can interview <u>in person</u> who is CURRENTLY WORKING in your chosen career. List the following information at the top of the page:
       the career you are pursuing,
       the person's name, title, name and address company where he/she works.
   d. Two Persons to Interview Homework Assignment
   e. Copy of the thank you letter in business format that you sent to the person you interviewed

6. Section 4: Sources

Be sure to cite any outside sources you have used in gathering your materials for this portfolio. A bibliography of publications and/or websites is needed as well as the names, titles, company names and addresses for the persons used for interviews or other information. A minimum of three sources must be cited. APA format for the citations is preferred.

8. The Drawbridge Exercise

DIRECTIONS: Please read the story completely. Then follow the instructions.

As he left for a visit to his outlying districts, the jealous Baron warned his pretty wife: "Do not leave the castle while I am gone, or I will punish you severely when I return!"

But as the hours passed the young Baroness grew lonely, and despite her husband's warning, decided to visit her lover who lived in the countryside nearby.

The castle was located on an island in a wide, fast flowing river, with a drawbridge linking the island on the land at the narrowest point in the river.

"Surely my husband will not return before dawn," she thought, and ordered her servants to lower the drawbridge and leave it down until she returned.

After spending several pleasant hours with her lover, the Baroness returned to the drawbridge, only to find it blocked by a madman wildly waving a long and crude knife.

"Do not attempt to cross this bridge, Baroness, or I will kill you," he raved.

Fearing for her life, the Baroness returned to her lover and asked him to help.

"Our relationship is only a romantic one," he said, "I will not help."

The Baroness then sought out a boatman on the river, explained her plight to him and asked him to take her across the river in his boat.

"I will do it, but only if you can pay my fee of five Marks."

"But I have no money with me!" the Baroness protested.

"That is too bad. No money, no ride," the boatman said flatly.

Her fear growing, the Baroness ran crying to the home of a friend, and after again explaining the situation, begged for enough money to pay the boatman his fee.

"If you had not disobeyed your husband, this would not have happened," the friend said. "I will give you no money."

With dawn approaching and her last resource exhausted, the Baroness returned to the bridge in desperation, attempted to cross to the castle and was slain by the madman.

DIRECTIONS: In the story there are six characters. They are (in alphabetical order):

The Baron _____   The Friend _____

The Baroness _____   The Lover _____

The Boatman _____   The Madman _____

Using the list above, rank the characters 1 through 6 in the order of their responsibility for the death of the Baroness. The rank of "1" holds the most responsibility.

Now, work with the other members of your group and decide on a **group** rank order for the six characters.

9. Grades, GPAs, Academic Honors

Students must complete all required work for courses by the last scheduled class. The only exception is if the course has been cancelled. At the end of each semester, students will receive a grade from the instructor for each course they enroll in. The grade indicates the level of achievement of the objectives of the course. Grades offered at Purdue Calumet are listed below. Please note that beginning with the Fall 2008 semester, the plus/minus grade option (B+/B/B-) will be available for assignment at the instructor's discretion.

THE FOLLOWING GRADING SCALE WILL BE USED:

A+, A	94–100%
A–	90–93%
B+	87–89%
B	84–86%
B–	80–83%
C+	77–79%
C	74–76%
C–	70–73%
D+	67–69%
D	64–66%
D–	60–63%
F	Below 60%

CALCULATING THE GPA:

The general formula for calculating a GPA is the weighted grade X semester hours = index points. The sum of all the index points divided by the number of semester hours is the GPA. A semester index GPA is an average of all of the index points for that semester; a cumulative GPA is an average of all of index points that the student has received

For the purpose of averaging, each grade shall be weighted and index points calculated as indicated.

Grade	Weight
A+, A	4.0 × semester hrs = index pts
A–	3.7 × semester hrs = index pts
B+	3.3 × semester hrs = index pts
B	3.0 × semester hrs = index pts
B–	2.7 × semester hrs = index pts
C+	2.3 × semester hrs = index pts
C	2.0 × semester hrs = index pts
C–	1.7 × semester hrs = index pts

D+	$1.3 \times$ semester hrs = index pts
D	$1.0 \times$ semester hrs = index pts
D–	$0.7 \times$ semester hrs = index pts
E,F,WF,EF,IF	$0.0 \times$ semester hrs = index pts
P,N,I,PI,SI,W	*Not included in GPA calculation*
WN,WU,IN,IU	*Not included in GPA calculation*

ACADEMIC HONORS

Dean's List: Each semester the Dean's List honors undergraduate students who have at least 12 credit hours in the graduation index with a graduate index of at least 3.5, and have at least six hours in the semester index of at least 3.0.

Students whose names are placed on the Dean's List shall be entitled to the following special privileges during the semester following the designation of distinction:

- May be assigned to more than 18 credit hours upon request.
- With the instructor's permission, a full-time Dean's List student may audit one class with assessment or additional fee.

Semester Honors: Semester Honors recognize undergraduate students who:

- Have at least six credit hours in the semester index with a semester index of at least 3.5 and
- Have at least a 2.0 graduation index.

If would be possible to earn both Dean's List and Semester Honors standing if the student has a really outstanding semester.

Note: Pass/no pass grades and credits in hour totals for either category of honors.

Sources: Academic Catalog, 2008–2009, pages 22 and 25; Plus/Minus grades information from a memo from VC for Academic Affairs dated 12/9/08.

CPSIA information can be obtained at www.ICGtesting.com
Printed in the USA
LVOW02s1911020715

444319LV00006B/15/P